Scattering the Dark

An Anthology of Polish Women Poets

Scattering the Dark

An Anthology of Polish Women Poets

Selected and edited by Karen Kovacik

WHITE PINE PRESS / BUFFALO, NEW YORK

P.O. Box 236
Buffalo, New York 14201
www.whitepine.org

Acknowledgments appear on pages 228-230, which constitute an extension of this copyright page.

Publication of this book was made possible, in part, by grants from the National Endowment for the Arts, which believes that a great nation deserves great art; the Polish Book Council: Instytut Książki-the ©POLAND Translation Programme, and with public funds from the New York State Council on the Arts, a State Agency.

Cover Design: Linda Maassen

First Edition

ISBN: 978-1-935210-82-5

Library of Congress Control Number: 2015943681

Contents

III. Reimagining the Bard

IV. The Ironic Art of Poetry

V. A Gallery of Myths and Masks

VI. Transitions, Transformations

VII. The Domestic Arts

VIII. Curating Objects

Introduction

The Polish word for Poland—*Polska*—is a feminine noun, and the country has traditionally been represented as a woman. This gendered figure arose when Poland ceased to exist as a nation after its partitioning by Russia, Prussia, and Austria in the late eighteenth century. The figure of the Polish motherland appeared as "a body in chains, in stocks, pushed into an open grave, even crucified," as feminist scholar Agnieszka Graff reminds us, and it was up to the country's Romantic poets—all men—to defend her and keep her alive. The legacy of this gendered figure has cast a long shadow. "Once the idea of a nation influences the perception of a woman," writes Eavan Boland about Ireland, a Catholic country whose history is in some ways analogous to Poland's, "she becomes the passive projection of a national idea." It would be an oversimplification to suggest that because women have functioned allegorically in the cultural imagination, actual women poets have been omitted from the literary canon. But except for a small "pantheon" —Nobel Laureate Wisława Szymborska (1922-2012), Julia Hartwig (b. 1921), Urzula Kozioł (b.1931), Krystyna Miłobędzka (b.1932), and Ewa Lipska (b.1945)—women poets time and again get omitted from the literary conversation. The work of their male peers becomes the basis for defining literary periods, schools, and movements.

As Kamila Pawluś has shown, Poland's women poets are underrepresented in the majority of mixed-gender anthologies and critical surveys of the nation's poetry. In seven recent anthologies, published in Poland, the United Kingdom, and United States, women poets' work comprised less that 15% on average. An anthology on the new Polish lyric (2011), edited by Jerzy Borowczyk and Michał Larek, included only one woman among twenty-eight poets. In critical surveys of postwar Polish poetry, women's poetry has also received scant attention. For instance, Jacek Gutorow's 2003 collection of sketches about Polish poetry since 1986 includes brief mention of only two women poets, overlooking even Wisława Szymborska, and his 2011 collection focuses on only three—and this, despite the fact, as Jerzy Jarniewicz, the well-known critic, translator, and poet, has argued, "the body of poetic works written by women poets is so significant that it would be easy to compile several substantial anthologies of excellent poems." Two earlier anthologies of women poets, published in the United States and Poland—Regina Grol's *Ambers Aglow* (1996) and Maria Cyranowicz et al.'s *Solistki* [Soloists] (2009)—featured poets who published their first collections before and after 1989, respectively. *Scattering the Dark* seeks connections among women writing before and after the fall of communism.

Poland's top two literary prizes—the Nike (a prize awarded to work of multiple genres, which has the stature of the Man Booker) and the Kościelski Foundation (awarded for outstanding poetic debuts) also go predominantly to men. In the seventeen years of the Nike's existence, four women have won, though many more have been nominated. For the Kościelski Prize, first awarded in 1962, of 134 laureates, only 16 have been women. Even when Wisława Szymborska was awarded the Nobel Prize in Literature in 1996, the Swedish Academy's decision was not without controversy in Poland because it meant that distinguished male poets of her generation—Zbigniew Herbert and Tadeusz Różewicz—would not win. Her biographers Anna Bikont and Joanna Szczęsna recorded headlines in Poland's conservative-leaning papers—"A Lesser Joy," "If Herbert Had Been a Woman" —that reflected this post-Nobel ambivalence.

Kamila Pawluś speculates that if Szymborska had not won the prize, few today in Poland would remember and write about her work.

As a corrective to what Benjamin Paloff has called the "men's club" of Polish literature in English, *Scattering the Dark* brings together thirty-one Polish women poets, born between 1909 and 1985, in a thematic arrangement. Instead of the chronological or alphabetical structures of many anthologies, these eight chapters juxtapose writers of different generations, regions, and sensibilities who write about similar subjects: history, dreams and the unconscious, Poland's tradition of bardic nationalism, the art of poetry itself, the advantages of using myths and masks, notions of home, life transitions, and objects as emblems. I derived these categories after studying some forty volumes by an array of Polish women poets, then looked for resonant poems in subsequent reading. Some poets are represented by a single poem; some appear in more than one chapter. While it is uncertain that one poem has directly influenced another, reading linked work by poets across generations allows us to hear correspondences, even when confronted with differences of style.

Connections across generations matter, given the profound changes Poland has undergone since its first free postwar elections in 1989 and, again, after it joined the European Union in 2004. The end of communism meant the eradication of government censorship and the return to civil liberties, giving way to freer travel abroad and more attention to the rights of ethnic, religious, and sexual minorities. But it also opened the country to global capitalism, and the abrupt transition from a full-employment, centrally planned economy to a free market had a dramatic impact on the lives of ordinary Poles. Poland's Catholic church, which had been allied with the political opposition during the communist era, now sought to protect its influence in a more secular, globalized world. The conservative Law and Justice Party, allied with the Church, continues to oppose civil reforms mandated by the European Union—such as reproductive freedom, gay marriage, and a 2015 statute against domestic violence—because they are perceived as threatening Polish identity by disrupting traditional gender roles.

On the literary scene, scores of new publishing houses and literary journals have cropped up, and in the first decade of the 21st century, many important poetry collections by women saw publication. Of course, the return to a market economy has also contributed to the commercialization of the publishing industry. Over the last fifteen years, in Poland's larger bookstores the shelves devoted to the country's poets have been crowded out by more populist fare. Polish critics, among them Marian Stala and Piotr Śliwiński, have lamented what they see as a generation gap among writers who first published before the fall of communism and those who made their debuts after. Poetry, once essential as bread, now is subject to the same market forces, the pressures for self-promotion as everywhere else. As early as 1986, Piotr Sommer, poet and editor of the influential journal *Literatura na świecie* [World Literature], had called for a "poetry of the everyday" in the manner of American poet Frank O'Hara to counter what he saw as the "values"-laden writing of earlier generations of poets, among them Czesław Miłosz and Zbigniew Herbert. And many writers, weary of poems focused on their country's traumatic history and politics, have embraced this poetics of the ordinary.

Some of the poets in this anthology have also responded critically to the traditional linking of national identity and poetry—what critics call the "Romantic paradigm"—and in particular, the belief that literature should serve the common good. Their targets tend to be Poland's Romantic poets, especially Adam Mickiewicz, and twentieth-century writers such as Miłosz, Herbert, and Leopold Staff, linked in the popular imagination, if not always in fact, with historical witness. Izabela Morska (b. 1961), for example, created the poetic alter ego, Madame Intuita—feminist, queer, and operating in a globalized world—in response to Zbigniew Herbert's earlier persona, Mr. Cogito, who tried to make rational sense of an irrational world under communism.

Yet despite Paloff's claim that Polish poets tend to become "rejectionists" after a decade or two of writing, we don't see the same noisy wrangling among Poland's female poets that we do among their male counterparts. Nobel Laureate Wisława Szymborska, even when privately criticized by some for her earlier membership in the communist party, has not become the target of polemics by younger poets as Miłosz and Herbert have. And Hartwig, Kozioł, and Miłobędzka have clearly mentored or inspired younger writers. Julia Hartwig, herself a distinguished translator, has often vetted English translations for Polish poets whose grasp of English is not as strong. And Urszula Kozioł, who has published many Polish poets in the influential journal *Odra,* generously suggested younger writers to include in *Scattering the Dark.* Krystyna Miłobędzka's minimalist poetry, full of resonant, sound-driven reinventions of common turns of phrase, has influenced the work of such poets as Julia Fiedorczuk, Agnieszka Mirahina, and Joanna Mueller.

Even given the dramatic changes Poland has seen in recent decades, the country's female poets have certain things in common. For one, they're a cosmopolitan group, influenced by extensive contacts with other literatures and languages. Szymborska translated French Baroque poetry; Hartwig has brought into Polish many French and American poets, including Apollinaire, Cendrars, Reverdy, Ginsberg, Moore, and Williams; Kozioł continues to edit *Odra*, which fostered crucial literary conversations with an international group of writers even during the communist era; Lipska directed the Polish Institute in Vienna; Kuciak won a prize for retranslating *The Divine Comedy*; Rodowska has brought many Francophone and Spanish-language poets in Polish, and is currently translating Proust. Some of the writers teach in departments of English or American studies, among them Chruściel, Fiedorczuk, and Morska. Chruściel, with Miłosz Biedrzycki, translated American poet Jorie Graham into Polish. Virtually all have participated in international literary festivals or exchanges. And all have had the experience of seeing their own work brought into other languages. Some write in more than one language or translate their own work. Ewa Parma who sometimes writes in English, then brings her work into Polish has described self-translation as a "lovely, creative schizophrenia."

Multilingual contact shows up in countless ways, not least in book or poem titles in a language other than Polish. Most of Bargielska's books have had English-language titles— *Bach for My Baby, China Shipping,* and *Dating Sessions*. Boruń-Jagodzińska's "Queen Kong," Morska's *Madame Intuita,* and Kozioł's *Horrendum* all have international resonance. This cosmopolitan quality also appears in allusions to writers from other languages—from Heraclitus to Maxine Hong Kingston. Subject matter and style have seen influences from wide reading and cultural exchange, as well. The adoption of personas from classical mythology, the Brothers Grimm, and biblical characters all connect this group of poets with archetypes and resonances beyond Poland's borders. Even as culture wars continue to play out in Poland—between a conservative, nationalistic version of the country's identity and a more international, outwardly focused one—this group of poets has absorbed significant cultural influences from abroad, while still being committed to Polish literature and its institutions.

Second, many of the included poems speak to gendered experience. In the history chapter, the poets challenge and supplement what Svetlana Alexievich calls "'male images and sensations of war," representing the impact of conflict or trauma on women and girls. Anna Swir writes from the perspective of an insurrectionary nurse during the Warsaw Uprising, Julia Hartwig's minimalist lyric "Some Women from Warsaw" shows the title characters conversing over coffee about their experiences of torture, and Wioletta Grzegorzewska juxtaposes the Chernobyl nuclear disaster with a girl's first menstrual period. In various chapters, we see the influence of Roman Catholicism in shaping the identity of girls and women but also clever ways of subverting Church authority. Krystyna Lenkowska's "An Overdue Letter to a Pimply Angel," in Ewa Hryniewicz-Yarbrough's translation, layers the Annunciation angel, Mary's virgin birth, and the speaker's own remembered passage through puberty to challenge female self-sacrifice. Julia Hartwig's "Escaping One's Chores" shows poets Wisława Szymborska, Urszula Kozioł and Ewa Lipska, charged with the drudgery of peeling potatoes and pitting cherries for jam, writing poems instead, tempted by "a skinny envoy of the daemon." In the myths and masks chapter, many of the writers use personas to express rage, frustration, or desire. Katarzyna Ewa Zdanowicz's Red Riding Hood poem, for example, indicts fear-mongering and victim-blaming in the culture's response to sexual violence: "don't cut through the woods / because they'll rape you / and forget to finish you off." In Izabela Morska's "Chrysalis," wearing men's clothing provides women camouflage for maneuvering through the patriarchy with élan.

But generational differences do exist. Poets who came of age after the fall of communism tend to include more explicitly autobiographical content, influenced by the "Personism" of poets like Frank O'Hara but also by more expressive tendencies within the Polish tradition—including some late poems by Anna Swir and Miłosz. This directness, for example, appears in "My Little Son Died" by Marzena Broda and in family poems by Joanna Wajs and Ewa Chruściel. Franker treatments of queer or lesbian desire are also a phenomenon of the post-communist scene, as in included poems by Izabela Morska and Agnieszka Mirahina. Another generational difference in the work of these writers—Morska, Mirahina, Bożena Keff, Julia Fiedorczuk, Joanna Mueller, Katarzyna Ewa Zdanowicz, and Ewa Chruściel—is the influence of post-structuralist theories of language, gender, and identity. And, not surprisingly, emblems of a globalized world, appear frequently in poems from the last decades: Sonnenberg's "Love Poem," with its motifs of consumer goods from a world marketplace, her "Signs of the Times," in which the muses have to prostitute themselves to live, and Morska's "Madame Intuita, Vampire-Killer…," with its representations of a seductive lesbian vampire in a media-saturated age. However, allusions to globalization do not only occur in the work of poets born after 1960. Kozioł's "To My Poem," Hartwig's "Inventory," and even Kuś's "Poem of the Seven Veils," a satire of the centrally planned economy during the communist era in the form of a striptease, all situate Poland's specificity in an international context.

In the post-communist era, Jewish-related topics have also received greater attention, particularly Polish-Jewish relations, responses to the Holocaust, and representations of anti-Semitism in

Poland both before and after the war. Bożena Keff's *Utwór o matce i ojczyźnie* [The Thing About Mother and Fatherland] (2008), a layered, genre-bending collection of poems, weaves together American blues songs, the Tomb Raider video game, and the Demeter-Persephone myth in its treatment of a mother who survived the Holocaust and her adult daughter. Though no excerpt can convey the operatic force of the entire collection, *Scattering the Dark* includes Keff's poem "Lara Croft" in a crisp translation by Benjamin Paloff and Alissa Valles. Other poems evoke the Holocaust by focusing on sites of "postmemory," Marianne Hirsch's term for how "traumatic memories of those who experienced the Holocaust are internalized by generations that come after them." Agnieszka Kuciak in "Wroniecka Street Pool" and Agnieszka Wolny-Hamkało in "Fragments of Maps" depict the fates of two different synagogues. Julia Hartwig's "In Transit," set in a Jewish cemetery, suggests that the past, as William Faulkner famously said, "is not past yet," that the trauma of the Holocaust and its legacy remain vividly imprinted in the collective consciousness.

The thematic structure of the anthology, then, allows us to hear conversations among Poland's women poets who came of age as writers both before and after the fall of communism. But it also illustrates differences in style and approach even among poets who treat similar subjects. While most of the poems in The Ironic Art of Poetry chapter are in free verse, Agnieszka Kuciak's sonnet "Meter" argues for traditional rhythm's ability to record change but also its tendency to be mastered by it. And even among poets writing in free verse, there's much formal variety—from Szymborska's highly end-stopped "The Joy of Writing," which extols the writer's ability to control the textual world, to Julia Hartwig's "The Sentence," which eschews punctuation in its search for a form that "envelops . . . formlessness," to Marzanna Kielar's "Manuscript," featuring bursts of natural images without capitalization as if to piece "together words / in a foreign tongue." Ewa Lipska's "Questions at a Poetry Reading" and "My Translators" make use of quick, associative leaps—hallmarks of her style—to explore difficulties of reception in both performance and translation.

As the editor of every anthology knows, the painful part is excluding writers for one reason or another. A number of poets did not fit within the thematic scheme, and some poems that sounded fresh in a Polish context simply did not make the leap in translation. Further, certain schools or styles of poetry present significant problems in translation. The neo-Language (*neolingwistyczny*) movement, much in vogue in Poland at the time of this writing, poses challenges because of its punning, sound-driven poetics, which often rely on culturally specific idioms or slang. In the Reimagining the Bard chapter, Joanna Mueller's "Proofreading," a neo-Language poem, questions the relevance of searching for errors—and, by extension, notions of literary value—in our increasingly untextual age. Mueller's original referred to features of Polish grammar, such as the requirement to use the seven grammatical cases correctly, which English does not have. But in translation I was able to find meaningful equivalents for the Anglophone reader, while also preserving the poem's music and punning. Surreal poems that frequently change voice or point of view—popular in Poland, as well—also present difficulties because they typically require a shared cultural background for readers to make meaning across ruptures or silences. The translator must parse what occurs on either side of such a leap and then find an equivalent in English, which often means selecting one interpretation over others and reducing the poem's resonance. My own editorial preferences for short lyrics, an ironic coolness of tone, and poems that in some way give voice to gendered concerns also influenced selection.

It was important to me from the outset to include the work of multiple translators, not only because each of us brings our own sensibility to the process of transferring a poem from one language to the other, but also because English as a global language comes in more than one variety. Translators living in Poland, the United Kingdom, and the United States all take into account the requirements of their different audiences. Szymborska's well-known translators Stanisław Barańczak and Clare Cavanagh, for instance, typically imbue their versions of her poems with a formal finesse. In "Stage Fright," which appears in chapter 4 of this anthology, Barańczak and Cavanagh slightly heighten the contrast between how the speaker would like to dress for a poetry reading and how she actually appears [emphasis mine]:

> If at least the dress were longer and more flowing
> and the poems appeared not from a *handbag* but by
>   *sleight of hand,*
> *dressed in their Sunday best* from head to toe,
> with bells on, ding to dong,
> ab ab ba —

The italicized phrase "by sleight of hand" in Polish is "wprost z rękawa"—literally, "straight from the sleeve" as in a magic trick—a resonance Barańczak and Cavanagh convey by substituting a different phrase from the illusionist's art ("by sleight of hand") to intensify the opposition with "not from a handbag." The internal rhyme in the phrase "*dressed* in their Sunday *best,*" which doesn't appear in the original, has a similar effect.

In "Some Women from Warsaw," my translation of Julia Hartwig's "Siedziały panie" [literally, "Some Women [or Ladies] Were Sitting"], found in the first chapter of this anthology, I introduced quotation marks where there were none in the original to emphasize the shifts from one speaker to another. Such shifts seemed important, given what I perceived as a competition among these women sitting over coffee to outdo one another in sharing experiences of intimidation, torture, or tragedy during the war.

In the end, I produced about sixty percent of the translations for the anthology, and I'm grateful to an A-list of Polish translators—Stanisław Barańczak, Daniel Bourne, Clare Cavanagh, John and Bogdana Carpenter, Robin Davidson, Piotr Florczyk, Ewa Hryniewicz-Yarbrough, Bill Johnston, Marek Kazmierski, Antonia Lloyd-Jones, Czesław Miłosz, Leonard Nathan, Ewa Elżbieta Nowakowska, Benjamin Paloff, Alissa Valles, Iza Wojciechowska, and Elżbieta Wójcik-Leese—for ensuring that the poetry retained its resonance, artfulness, and wit in English. Thanks, too, to Ela Wójcik-Leese, Izabela Morska, and Kamila Pawluś for their helpful editorial suggestions on an earlier version of the manuscript. Jim Powell and Ewa Hryniewicz-Yarbrough offered generous commentary on the introduction and chapter headnotes, and Bill Johnston's endorsement led to grants from Indiana University and the IUPUI Arts and Humanities Institute that supported work on this project. I would also like to thank Dennis Maloney of White Pine Press; Robert Hass, Edward Hirsch, and Valzhyna Mort for their votes of confidence; Mira Kuś for supplying the title; Erica E. Harris for the cover image; and Linda Maassen for adapting Erica's image to a Polish context. Finally, I'm especially grateful to all thirty-one participating poets.

—Karen Kovacik
Indianapolis

About the Text

When available, I've included dates of composition and first publication immediately after each poem, and translators' names also appear at poem's end. Because the book is designed for the general reader, I've eliminated scholarly parenthetical references and most of the notes, except when necessary to provide historical or literary context. But readers interested in delving into the source materials for this book will find works cited and consulted in the bibliography. All quotations from Polish-language texts in the introduction and chapter headnotes appear in my translation unless otherwise indicated.

— K.K.

I. Lifting the Veils of History

In *The Witness of Poetry* (1983), Czesław Miłosz famously remarked, "The true home of the Polish poet is history." Even now some Western readers still associate Polish poetry with historical witness, not realizing that younger generations of writers tend to reject this reckoning with their country's difficult past. Such readers recall Miłosz's devastating poems about Warsaw in World War II, Tadeusz Różewicz's *Poetry of Survival,* Anna Swir's stark lyrics on the Warsaw Uprising, Zbigniew Herbert's "Report from a Besieged City," composed after the imposition of Martial Law in 1981, or perhaps Adam Zagajewski's "Going to Lvov," an elegiac homage to his native city, which became part of the Soviet Union just after the poet's birth and necessitated a permanent exile.

The poets in this chapter tend to present Poland's complicated history from apocryphal perspectives, often with a gendered slant. As Clare Cavanagh has observed, "Certainly Poland's experience of seeing its own history rewritten time and again by one conquering nation or another has sensitized its writers to the ways in which individuals and peoples alike may be revised or deleted entirely by official chroniclers past and present." In these poems, the focus tends to be on women and girls, and this slight shifting of the lens creates some surprising effects. The chapter opens with Wisława Szymborska's evocation of what Germans call the *Trümmerfrauen*, rubble-women, charged with cleaning up the aftermath of war. Szymborska's point is clear: if we emphasized the mess of "after" rather than the heroics of "before," we might postpone the rush to war. Julia Hartwig's "Victoria" depicts a young Polish woman, perhaps a version of the poet, right after the war when the Soviet army comes to "liberate" the country. Unlike Poland's allies celebrating with champagne and kisses, this narrator feels ambivalent—grateful the war is over, fearful of the Soviet occupation to come.

This chapter's poets help us think about history differently in part through their use of personas. Szymborska's "Hitler's First Photograph," centered around an infant picture of the Führer, occurs largely in baby talk, as guests gather to wish the newborn well and to imagine his future as a tenor in the Viennese opera or the husband of the Bürgermeister's daughter—bourgeois dreams blissfully ignorant of the history to come. Skipping ahead several decades, Ewa Lipska's "Confessions of a Courtesan" has the title character commenting on the foibles and phobias of her powerful Communist Party clients. Krystyna Miłobędzka's poem takes the form of a different sort of confession—the kind one might make to the secret police or a priest—simultaneously conveying how even the most ordinary objects might appear dangerous to the authorities and implicating language's inability to resist the status quo. Mira Kuś's "Poem of the Seven Veils" sends up the absurdities of a centrally planned economy through a striptease. She pokes fun at the politicized rhetoric of that era in the encyclopedia entry of section one; the selection of street names in section three; the factory surrealism, riffing on André Breton, in the fourth; or even the curious acronym "Pewex," short for "Import-Export Company," a chain of hard-currency stores where one could buy otherwise unattainable goods for dollars, Deutschmarks and pounds—an institution Franz Kafka might have dreamed up. The centrally planned economy affects even something as intimate as buying underwear.

Images of Jewish Poland and allusions to the Holocaust occur in a number of the poems. Bożena Keff's "Lara Croft," excerpted from *The Thing About Mother and Fatherland,* suggests the fraught relationship between a mother who survived the Holocaust and her adult daughter, likened to the Tomb Raider video game's heroine. In this poem, the mother, decades after the war, discovers documentation of her own mother's execution in a forest, and the daughter struggles to find words other than the stock expressions of sympathy we might expect from the Croft character. Agnieszka Wolny-Hamkało and Agnieszka Kuciak describe the fates of former synagogues in the cities of Wrocław and Poznań, desecrated by the German army during World War II. Wolny-Hamkało's title "Fragments of Maps" suggests the tiny shreds of historical memory that threaten to be forgotten. Her poem depicts a nighttime ballet lesson in a former synagogue that has recently become a Jewish cultural center. Kuciak's poem about a Poznań synagogue converted by the Wehrmacht to a swimming hall for soldiers, which remained a city pool until 2012, speaks to the intimate transmission of historical memory when a mother informs her son learning to swim of the building's original sacred purpose.

In fact, the experience of history in these poems is visceral, registered in the body. The Chernobyl nuclear disaster gets conflated with a girl's first menstrual period in Wioletta Grzegorzewska's "Spring, 1986." Women sitting over coffee in Julia Hartwig's postwar café poem talk not of trivial matters but of torture, death and destruction. "They ripped off my fingernails," says one.

Agnieszka Mirahina, only four years old in 1989 when the first free postwar elections were held in Poland, evokes the cadence, tone, and distorted syntax of Soviet propaganda broadcasts. Her poem hints at the Katyń Forest massacre of Polish officers by the Soviet secret police in 1940, the Orwellian doublespeak both confirming the atrocity and denying responsibility for it. The collage form of her poem and the phrase "jazz has broken through the floor below" remind us that the freewheeling improvisational genre was branded "cosmopolitan" and "bourgeois" by the Soviet authorities immediately after World War II. Listening to it on a Western radio station was a counter-revolutionary activity during the Stalinist years.

The final poem in the chapter, Ewa Lipska's "Freedom," in only six lines, conveys specific qualities of post-communist Poland—its wish to be considered part of Europe, the wealth and political power of the Catholic Church, which seeks to preserve Poland from secular and global influences that it sees as threatening the nation's identity. During the communist era, the Church allied itself with the political opposition, keeping certain kinds of historical memory alive and even allowing uncensored literary readings, theatrical performances, and art exhibits in places of worship. In recent decades, the Church has played a more conservative role in Polish culture, allying itself with the nationalist Law and Justice party and opposing the civil rights reforms mandated by the country's membership in the European Union. In Lipska's poem, the image of the "streets [lying] prostrate in crosses" calls into question the meaning of an abstraction like "freedom."

Wisława Szymborska

The End and the Beginning

After every war
someone has to tidy up.
Things won't pick
themselves up, after all.

Someone has to shove
the rubble to the roadsides
so the carts loaded with corpses
can get by.

Someone has to trudge
through sludge and ashes,
through the sofa springs,
the shards of glass,
the bloody rags.

Someone has to lug the post
to prop the wall,
someone has to glaze the window,
set the door in its frame.

No sound bites, no photo opportunities,
and it takes years.
All the cameras have gone
to other wars.

The bridges need to be rebuilt,
the railroad stations, too.
Shirtsleeves will be rolled
to shreds.

Someone, broom in hand,
still remembers how it was.
Someone else listens, nodding
his unshattered head.
But others are bound to be bustling nearby
who'll find all that
a little boring.

From time to time someone still must
dig up a rusted argument
from underneath a bush
and haul it off to the dump.

Those who knew
what this was all about
must make way for those
who know little.
And less than that.
And at last nothing less than nothing.

Someone has to lie there
in the grass that covers up
the causes and effects
with a cornstalk in his teeth,
gawking at clouds.

Translated by Stanisław Barańczak and Clare Cavanagh

Wisława Szymborska

Hitler's First Photograph

And who's this little fellow in his itty-bitty robe?
That's tiny Adolf, the Hitlers' little boy!
Will he grow up to be an L.L.D.?
Or a tenor in the Vienna Opera House?
Whose tummy full of milk, we just don't know:
printer's, doctor's, merchant's, priest's?
Where will these tootsie-wootsies finally wander?
To a garden, to a school, to an office, to a bride?
Maybe to the Bürgermeister's daughter?

Precious little angel, mommy's sunshine, honey bun.
While he was being born, a year ago,
there was no dearth of signs on the earth and in the sky:
spring sun, geraniums in windows,
the organ-grinder's music in the yard,
a lucky fortune wrapped in rosy paper.
Then just before the labor his mother's fateful dream.
A dove seen in a dream means joyful news—
if it is caught, a long-awaited guest will come.
Knock knock, who's there, it's Adolf's heartchen knocking.

A little pacifier, diaper, rattle, bib,
our bouncing boy, thank God and knock on wood, is well,
looks just like his folks, like a kitten in a basket,
like the tots in every other family album.
Sh-h-h, let's not start crying, sugar.
The camera will click from under that black hood.

The Klinger Atelier, Grabenstrasse, Braunau.
And Braunau is a small, but worthy town—
honest businesses, obliging neighbors,
smell of yeast dough, of gray soap.
No one hears howling dogs, or fate's footsteps.
A history teacher loosens his collar
and yawns over homework.

Translated by Stanisław Barańczak and Clare Cavanagh

Julia Hartwig

Victoria

Why didn't I dance on the Champs-Élysées
when the crowd cheered the end of the war?
Why didn't I throw myself into the arms of a sailor
who walked down the gangway with a duffel on his arm
and ran toward me through the excited crowd
raging sounds of bebop
"*La Marseillaise*" and "God Save the Queen"
blaring from the loudspeakers?

Why didn't I break out a bottle of champagne
next to the two of them still dressed in English uniforms
not guessing one day I would stand at the end of their road?

Why was I fated to be on the main street of Lublin
watching regiments with red stars enter the city
crying with joy I would no longer hear the hated *Raus!* and *Halt!*
but torn by sadness this was the price of a lost dream
of a hero's triumphant entry on a white horse
for the return of those who twice cheated
didn't want to come back

So we stood—the ones who survived—
on the streets of Warsaw transformed into a desert
and today years later find ourselves
in the fading films of newsreels
hard to recognize

(2003, 2004) *Translated by John and Bogdana Carpenter*

Julia Hartwig

Some Women from Warsaw

Some women were sitting over coffee.
"They ripped off my fingernails," said one.
"I had a floodlight trained on me."
"For two days they dribbled me with water."
"They ruptured my kidneys."
"They shot my son and burned my father."
Some ordinary women from Warsaw.

(published 1969)

Translated by Karen Kovacik

Anna Swir

I Carried Bedpans

I worked as an orderly at the hospital
without medicine and water.
I carried bedpans
filled with pus, blood and feces.

I loved pus, blood and feces—
they were alive like life,
and there was less and less
life around.

When the world was dying,
I was only two hands, handing
the wounded a bedpan.

(1974) *Translated by Piotr Florczyk*

Julia Hartwig

This Is How It Will Be

It will all return
There will be no ashes or rubble
everything restored like before the devastation
in sunlight and full bloom

Friendships not marred by quarrels
wells not poisoned
battlefields where the hope for victory remains

The stars uncounted
the moon not yet explored
and us still unaware
of what could transpire
and what will be taken
from us forever

(published 2007)

Translated by Karen Kovacik

Julia Hartwig

In Transit

The oldest trees
are in the Jewish cemetery

The raven
mute cantor
doesn't sing

Above the treetops
they swarm by the thousands
a heavy autumn cloud

Come out to meet them all of you
locked in this mansion of monuments

Go together
through lightning
and lashing rain

Those who have no place
who are themselves fire and rain
will keep you company

Since the end of their end
has not yet come
to an end

(published 2004)

Translated by Karen Kovacik

Bożena Keff

Lara Croft

Narratrix
In the backwaters of depression she lies half-sunk, her open maw
full of complaint—sometimes a tongue of hot lava—sometimes
          a scattering
of cold ash from the archives of the Jewish Historical Institute,
where, sorting through the shot and the gassed,
she stumbles on something.
"I found," says she, looking
straight into the void (which is me, on a chair), "a document.
My mother was killed in a forest outside Lvov.
She was shot in the forest. Half a century, and I didn't know."

*

For half a century she didn't know, and now she knows.
And she speaks of it in the presence of a random witness.
In point of fact, a brunette in crocodile-skin gloves,
agent from the world of make-believe, Lara Croft, or some such,
who's firing up her Cessna in Hawaii when an old maid
in a threadbare cloak gets snagged in the propeller. Lara climbs out
to help the poor thing, who, gazing into the void, informs her
that half a century ago her mother was shot in the forest.

"How horrible!"
cries Lara, for she is not without heart.

(published in 2008)

Translated by Benjamin Paloff and Alissa Valles

Agnieszka Wolny-Hamkało

Fragments of Maps

The White Stork Synagogue
had swelled on every side, slightly
ruffled by the moon—because inside, in the courtyard, there were no
lamps.
Where was that industrial light coming from?
We suddenly realized: upstairs
there was a glass-walled room and a ballet lesson. At night?
We stood confined in the dark courtyard,
watching the soundless show.
A glass ball with something white inside
that spun like underlit snow.

(2005, 2007)

Translated by Bill Johnston

Agnieszka Kuciak

Wroniecka Street Pool

In swimming class, he hears: "Don't go too deep."
His lips feel withered from the harsh chlorine.

Against his palms the water pushes back;
It folds around his body like a Hasid's cloak.

With tranquil, fluid strokes, his shoulders whip
Through the water's faded pages, as if

He'd like to ask: "Mother, why does that school
Of shadows glisten at the bottom of the pool?"

"In dreams and in this pool, sometimes the dead
Arise, and the water calls for them to be fed.

They're ghosts, who showered once beneath a wall
Of tears, and then when cleansed, they stole

Back home. At night, they take the baths
That they were promised in the camp.

So, son, swim quietly. Their echoes still resound
Here in this shrine, but they blame no one.

Swimming, we keep folding and opening our palms
As if in prayer, like when we say the psalms

And measure with each breath like scripture verse
This sacred space (the roof's yarmulke in place)."

(1996, 2001) *Translated by Karen Kovacik*

Ewa Lipska

Confessions of a Courtesan

"Most are afraid of the light," she says,
fastening her black garter, "and the people."
She opens her cigarette case. "And accomplices."
She props her leg on the bed frame.
"They're suspicious, they check behind the curtains.
They invite me to parachute jumps,
to bulletproof cocktails in secluded bars.
They call on me in emergencies.
I have lots of keepsakes. Photos.
Medals. Newspapers.
The one on the left died. This one was shot.
Officially I run
a bridal boutique.
These gowns have survived many revolutions.
They've witnessed coups of love.
In some you can still hear
hearts flutter. Frilly white cages."
She touches up the blush on her cheeks.
"Over time they lose their luster
and slip off the shoulder" —she lights a cigarette—
"and one general," she adds,
"just to amuse me
ate all his insignia
and stayed till morning.
We like clients like that
in these apathetic times

when the black swan in your eye
means ill fate."

(published 1985)

Translated by Robin Davidson and Ewa Elżbieta Nowakowska

Krystyna Miłobędzka

I remember (jottings under martial law)

I confess the hairpins

brass buttons

wrist chain

ballpoint pen

iron bars in my head

steel hoop gripping my heart (how these words rust)

helicopter in my eyes

tanks in my dreams

I don't remember any other scrap metal

(I have sinned)

(1982, 1992) *Translated by Elżbieta Wójcik-Leese*

Mira Kuś

Poetry of the Seven Veils

I
I begin with my boots.
What boots look like everyone knows,
but after one or two seasons such boots
will be the stuff of memory,
and in the winter of '83 or '84
you'll find them in the encyclopedia under B: Butt,
Isaac (1813-79), Ir. politician, leader of a movement
for the home rule of Ireland while maintaining
union with England. Barefoot
against your will, losing your shoes,
you land in politics.

II
My coat.
(Forget about it.)
It hangs on a hanger—I'll take up my blouse instead.
Dark brown, soft, polyester, '77 A.D.
Sporty, fragrant, freshly washed (a half kilo of detergent
for each member of the Polish Writers' Association),
the cuffs and collar slightly frayed.
Directing the reader's gaze
to the slow unbuttoning of buttons
I slip it off in a flash
so no one sees the rip. The gesture
is fast yet smooth, and your gaze
drifts over the crook of my arm,
flits to my shoulder, lands on my head and neck,

lights on my now unnecessary blouse—
and there gets stuck.

III
The lowest things
are no worse than the highest.
So as not to demoralize the masses
I remove my well-traveled stockings—7 Mikołajska Street,
4 Independence Avenue, 2 Rakowicka, 5 Myśliwiecka,
86 Heroes of Stalingrad Blvd., 3 Prince Janusz Ln., 9 Gagarin, 7 Cross St. —
then darn the holes and snags.

IV
Let us praise the masses buffeted by work, pleasure, or revolt,
the colorful, polyphonic tides of revolution in modern capitals,
vibrating with the feverish nights of arsenals and shipyards set ablaze
by violent moons; insatiable train stations; cloud-drenched factories
tied to the spiralling twine of their smoke, bridges
like giant gymnasts; hotheaded ships prowling
the horizon; barrel-chested locomotives
and slippery planes in flight. Let us praise the worker
gripping the wheel whose ideal axle
pierces the earth—my nerves can't take it:
I slip my skirt over my head.

V
A wonder of pink silk, rejected for export,
in a froth of embroidery and lace.
Sliver of cake on a porcelain plate.
Peppermint candy.
Wild strawberry in a swirl of cream.
Blushing daisy, raspberry ice
in clouds of vanilla custard.
A dessert for dreamers. A work of art,
pret à porter. This chemise,

my body longs for it
at eight dollars and fifty cents
beyond the window of a Pewex.

VI
Decorum suggests I mention
it's time now for underwear.
But here, where daily reality
smacks you in the face,
who thinks about the nether regions
of the body? With a desperate shrug,
I remove my bra.
Yeah... Well, times have changed. At least,
I'm not suggesting the West is to blame,
though despite our decades of hard work,
the economy's in the tank.
And why mention the exulting
beneath the Statue of Liberty
when after their shipment of imperialist chickens
our broilers gave up the ghost?
Instead of cutlets, we'll have bullshit.
And women will be assigned to stripping feathers.

VII
It's finally time for new underwear.
Panties with castoff slogans: *I love you, sweetheart,*
Cupid with his bow. Everything gnawed on
by the jaws of time. Panties—that is, the idea of panties—
"frivolous," some would say "marvelous," though in reality,
scraps of fabric attached to my hips
with industrial-strength string—
our peasant existence in a nutshell.
Confused notions, satanic urges,
the wailing and gnashing of teeth, a full-time demon on staff. And now
with one quick tug my ragged (yet clean) underpants are exposed.

—Oh, Lord, leave me a shred of illusion
about this one part of my body at least,
that even if it lands in hot water, it's still all mine,
not yet collectivized,
riding on my two strong legs.

(1976, 1978)

Translated by Karen Kovacik and Mira Kuś

Wioletta Grzegorzewska

Spring, 1986

The night was heavy, but the air was alive.
—Mike Oldfield

At night, the Chernobyl cloud fell
on our pastures. Thyroids swelled.
The pond glowed with murmuring iodine,
swallows kissing crooked mirrors.

The radio kept playing "Moonlight Shadow."
In the barn, a girl scout from the city started
a club for virgins. Smoking menthols,
we took our lessons in preparing
for conjugal life from copies of *Playboy.*

There would be no other end to the world,
and yet it kept repeating, like cramps
and acne, till I discovered
spots of dark blood in my underwear.

(2011, 2011) *Translated by Marek Kazmierski*

Agnieszka Mirahina

All the Radio Stations of the Soviet Union

this is Moscow calling   all radio stations of the Soviet Union are working
this is Moscow calling

in the beginning was the word that marshaled armies divisions regiments
it named then swept away the ants   grim infantry of this earth

after the word came a convoy of brooms shovels chutes ovens
secrets going up in smoke

or rumbling over the mountains and through the woods to the dump

and no one really knows who purged the truth from that fairy tale
since the ants had always been here   had remained in Asia   this is
Moscow calling

each word's an order in the grammar of crackles hisses static
all radio stations of the Soviet Union are working

jazz has broken though the floor below   does the soul oven exist
the crematorium burns with curiosity

on the last night the darkness will catch fire and the ants will defect to our
side
this is Moscow calling   all radio stations of the Soviet Union are working

the last bullet's for us   this word's an order   jazz has broken through the
floor below

in the beginning was the word and it was used against you

all radio stations of the Soviet Union are working

(2007, 2008)

Translated by Karen Kovacik

Ewa Lipska

Freedom

My country roams through freedom.
Pretends to be Europe.

The streets lie prostrate in crosses.

A pilgrimage of waiters
carries the Holy Button on a collection plate.

(published 2007)

Translated by Robin Davidson and Ewa Elżbieta Nowakowska

II. In the Theater of Dreams

The poems in this chapter narrate voyages of dreams, splicing images from nature and culture and drawing on elemental landscapes filled with characters living and dead. To render a dreamscape in language is both performance and interpretation with broader cultural implications. As Helen Groth and Natalya Lusty have observed, "The importance of the dream is not simply what it tells of the individual's psychological life, but what it discloses about the psychic dimensions of all political and cultural life."

A number of the poems signal this communication between the personal and cultural through the longstanding analogy between dreams and cinema. The oneiric content of films makes them fitting vehicles for representing the surreal or uncanny. Joanna Lech's cinematic "Cuts" splices together images that accrue symbolic weight when considered together, initiating the speaker into the mysteries of violence, sex, gender, and death. Boys "waging war against milk and cats" are represented by "knives and sneakers left on the grass." Women washing clothes at the river are associated with "bloodstains on the sheets." Little girls "play house, princesses in white aprons." A child paging through a picture book with his father encounters not just animals like an elephant and a giraffe but also "poisonous mushrooms and hemp leaves." Each stanza of the poem represents a different gendered lesson.

Other poems contrast different cultural experiences with the world of dreams to sketch anarchic fears and desires. Agnieszka Wolny-Hamkało's "Black" freshens the familiar analogy between night and death. The suddenness of death "pushes into the air like helium, / canceling out all those slender pedestrians / like a ninja with a black marker." And Justyna Bargielska's "In this season, at this time of day" opens with the provocative line: "No, sweetie, I have to cut up the prostitute by myself." Throughout, the poem counterpoises stereotypical expectations for women—sweet terms of endearment, a betrothal, the female speaker's "admission / of ignorance on every subject"—with an aggressive rage, which extends not only to the prostitute but also to the male lover the speaker imagines dead, dreaming herself in a widow's long black dress. Dream imagery in such poems allows the writers to evoke the taboo, the uncanny, lurking beneath the veneer of decorum.

Given that dreams offer us ways to confront our fears, it's not surprising that the last century's turbulent history would make an appearance in them. As Walter Benjamin once noted, "Dreams have started wars, and wars, from the very earliest times, have determined the propriety and impropriety of dreams." At first glance, Szymborska's "In Praise of Dreams" extols the high culture abilities that dreaming affords us: painting like Vermeer, speaking fluent Greek, writing epics, playing the piano with "brilliance." But near the end, the poem turns, and still maintaining the light tone, the speaker drops in an allusion to Poland's history: "It's gratifying that I can always / wake up before dying. // As soon as war breaks out, / I roll over on my other side." Being able to evade war is an art akin to speaking Greek or painting domestic interiors like Vermeer. Similarly, Krystyna Dąbrowska's poem imagines "a travel agency for the dead," which allows even those who met a violent end to fly via the dreams of the living

Urszula Kozioł's "Under the Cover of Night" also presents a dreamscape from the aftermath of war:

> As a child right after the war I dreamed
> I was a soldier
> who returns to a deserted, ransacked house
> and knows that he has lost someone but can't remember who.
> Beyond an overturned chair he notices a grand piano
> sits down at it and begins to play
> something so terribly sad
> that in the morning right after opening my eyes
> I still hear an echo of that melody

Dreaming and poetry help her compose a dirge for all that was lost in the war and enter the imaginative worlds of others. Another poem fusing history and dream, Krystyna Lars' "I Dreamed I Collaborated…" is written from the point of view of "Joanna S.," a Solidarity activist from the city of Stalowa Wola in southeastern Poland, during the communist era. Using gothic imagery and language, Joanna S describes the consummate nightmare: collaborating with the secret police. By slowing down time and registering minute sensations in the body, Lars is able to evoke the magnitude of this imagined betrayal. For Kozioł and Lars, as for Walter Benjamin, "dreams take their meaning from their location in time and place and this is the key to their significance for cultural memory." Dream poems thus function as a kind of hidden archive in the culture.

In some poems, that archive spans water and land to signal the cusp between life and death or between the unconscious and conscious worlds. Marzanna Kielar's untitled poem opens with a catalogue of liminal images: a "frosted apple tree," a cumulus cloud whose peak looks like an anvil, its leaves whirling "in the smoke of mists." These figments, swirling in and out of view like a fog, suggest both life arrested and death as fodder for new growth. Marzena Broda, in "My Little Son Died," is only able to convey the inexpressibility of such a loss in images of dissolving in streams, waterfalls, and clouds—the fluid element that Jung associated with emotion. And in Joanna Lech's "The Tide Coming In," the sleeping daughter is a transitional figure—"like a fish flung onto the shore"—when she dreams of the dead. She becomes "a vessel, a black hole, [who] absorb[s] everything." This childlike and feminine receptivity, while threatening the integrity of the rational self, is something the girl's mother would like to emulate. Julia Fiedorczuk's "Lands and oceans" sees the body and landscape in textual terms: the "sea a stubborn subtext" and the solid body made mutable through its tears—the "salt . . . on the tongue's tip and . . . the dot over the i."

Poems about dreams offer ways to imagine what lies beyond limits of conscience and identity. Poet and critic Katarzyna Ewa Zdanowicz, whose work appears in Chapter 6 of this anthology, said in a 2014 interview: "Without a doubt [in Poland], there's a stereotype of women's writing: sentimental, hysterical, a bit schoolmarmish, and, above all, monothematic. . . . But consider instead Julia Kristeva's inspiring concept of matriarchal language: one of rebellion, intuition, imagination." Given lingering stereotypes of women's poetry in Poland, dream poems fill in the shadows of aggression, transgressive desire and terror that traditional notions of gender or poetry would overlook.

Joanna Lech

Cuts

Silence. It was supposed to be a tight shot, but the boys have slipped from
the frame.
They're waging war against milk and cats, and they're already late.
So let knives and sneakers left on the grass set the scene.

This time nothing gets reflected in the sun. Dusk is falling
and the women at the river will take up their laundry.
Let bloodstains on the sheets stand for sunset, story, everything.

Nearby, little girls play house, princesses in white aprons.
You'll become what you pretend, they squeal with fear, when I want to be a witch
from another tale. Let all of it unfold through images

instead of touch. The child in the armchair is turning pages.
That's an elephant, that's a giraffe, he tells his dad, though poisonous
mushrooms
and hemp leaves fall from the book. *You won't outrun decay,* whisper the wings

of moths. I don't recognize myself in the scene when the light changes.
I wriggle my fingers in the grass. Let the world shrink to fit our eyes—
where traps lie and lapping can be heard, the cat's tongue darting over a
knife.

(2007, 2008)

Translated by Karen Kovacik

Agnieszka Wolny-Hamkało

Black

Night springs up suddenly,
pushes into the air like helium,
its black marker crossing out
all those pedestrians slight as ninjas.

Night begins behind the scenes,
in a wig shop, in that letter from J. to A.,
in the curse your dream flings at you.
In the spot on an X-ray.

(2005, 2007) *Translated by Karen Kovacik*

Justyna Bargielska

In this season, at this time of day

No, sweetie, I have to cut up the prostitute by myself.
But thanks anyway. I loved you when you were but
a promise of yourself, though before that pledge
can be fulfilled, I have to carve up the prostitute
by myself. And don't get mad,
but I've got to be totally alone
when cutting her up. This glorious light,
like in a painting, the sailboats aglow, and my admission
of ignorance on every subject:
all this awaits you. The dream in which the mountains
and lake reflect the setting sun, and I'm swimming
in the lake in a long black dress,
black not for my children or parents,
but for you: all this awaits.
But really, I've got to do her
by myself. If you don't find that
in Purcell or Shostakovich,
and surely you won't,
look a little lower, in December, in the forest.

(2012, 2013) *Translated by Karen Kovacik*

Wisława Szymborska

In Praise of Dreams

In my dreams
I paint like Vermeer van Delft.

I speak fluent Greek
and not just with the living.

I drive a car
that does what I want it to.

I am gifted
and write mighty epics.

I hear voices
as clearly as any venerable saint.

My brilliance as a pianist
would stun you.

I fly the way we ought to,
i.e., on my own.

Falling from the roof,
I tumble gently to the grass.

I've got no problem
breathing under water.

I can't complain:
I've been able to locate Atlantis.

It's gratifying that I can always
wake up before dying.

As soon as war breaks out,
I roll over on my other side.

I'm a child of my age,
but I don't have to be.

A few years ago,
I saw two suns.

And the night before last a penguin,
clear as day.

Translated by Stanisław Barańczak and Clare Cavanagh

Krystyna Dąbrowska

Travel Agency

I am a travel agency for the dead,
I book them flights to the dreams of the living.
Famous celebrities apply to me, like Heraclitus,
to be able to visit a writer who's in love with him,
but so do the lesser-known dead – like a farmer from Wasiły village,
wishing to advise his wife on matters of rabbit breeding.
Sometimes several generations of a family charter an airplane
and land on the brow of their final descendant.
I also have dealings with the murdered,
who on regular trips to the dreams of the survivors,
collect up points in a frequent flyer program.
I never deny my services to anyone.
I find them the very best connections
and I reproach myself when a young lover,
to get into his girlfriend's dream,
must make a transfer in the dream of a snoring crone.
Or when weather conditions force an emergency landing
and the dead man calls me: do something,
I'm stuck in the dream of a terrified child!
Incidents like these mean stress and a challenge
for me, a minor business with major ambitions –
for though I have no access either to the dead men's world
or into other peoples' dreams,
thanks to me they come in contact.

(2006, 2006) *Translated by Antonia Lloyd-Jones*

Urszula Kozioł

Under the Cover of Night

Under the cover of night I forget about my life
I go to unfamiliar places
and though I'm nearly the person I've always been
I become someone else
and even change sex.

As a child right after the war I dreamed
I was a soldier
who returns to a deserted, ransacked house
and knows that he has lost someone but can't remember who.
Behind an overturned chair he notices a grand piano
sits down at it and begins to play
something so terribly sad
that in the morning
right after opening my eyes
I still hear an echo of that melody

and just then I remember
I have no idea how to play
any instrument

but if I do
it's only under the cover of night
when my "I" turns into someone else.

(published 2010)

Translated by Karen Kovacik

Krystyna Lars

"I Dreamed I Collaborated," Says Joanna S., Solidarity Activist from Stalowa Wola

I did it. I signed.
When I took the pen in hand, eternity cracked open
a window. From the street I could hear a vacuum explode. That blank
page — it was supposed to land without a sound. From stacks of paper
helicopters lifted off, dropping a black rain
of words. On my hands, pink welts. Full
of barbed letters, my heart hurt. Leaded lines of type
pushed through my veins, beveled like the edges
of knives. Titles red as sunsets rimmed
my lids. Predatory inscriptions climbed the rungs
of my retina. My eye gaped like a stadium,
a huge score clock for a match between fire
and air, lashes whipping like pennants.
Thousands of torches shone in regular rows. Flecks of white
around the papilla at the pupil's core. Clouds tipped
card files of air over the grandstand. White questionnaires
swirling in the wind were mistaken for doves.
In tunnels, my blood stalled like trolleys. Night fell.
I felt calm. I kept my thoughts to myself. Only
I couldn't stomach the disgrace. Pen nibs,
paper clips, wire signature coils, sacramental ink
for stamping stuck in my craw…
At last my blankness was filled in.
Without fanfare, I came to. They told me
I could collect my things
and go home.

(1990, 1991) *Translated by Karen Kovacik*

Joanna Lech

Postscript

Back behind the train station lie ruins of houses, shattered windows, trash.
A broken swing.
Nothing's here, nothing's left, the tracks are overgrown. So I don't
understand
what you're doing, twirling around, holding out your hands.

Maybe you're still trying to catch something: that certain moment,
the furrowed sky, yourself
in the photo? But there's nothing here. Nothing stops at this deserted
station,
these empty benches and platforms, a forest round the bend. Nothing's
here,

I repeat, when you reach up and the light flakes from your fingers,
those last shimmering scraps, so hard to freeze, so hard to grasp.

(2008, 2008) *Translated by Karen Kovacik*

Marzanna Kielar

***

Like an oxidized breath, mist from a mouth,
this frosted apple tree, at the back, near the greenhouse door—
it's the earth that speaks at the cooled-down daybreak.

It's the clouds that speak, parted by strips of clear sky.
Cumulus approaching from the horizon: its peak an anvil,
a heavy storm collar at its base.

Day tightens the mooring chains of the town, its crust of ice glints.
It carries us in a sprawling roll.
Then slowly hauls the flapping net, unloads it onto a ship
that will never return.

Leaves speak in dreams, in the smoke of mists, "Pick your steps
 cautiously.
The skin of the earth, look, is all made of bodies we used to be."

But the dead remain silent.
They dig shafts in the air on cloudless, leafless nights.
Drink our breaths over the switched-off town
revolving at its anchor.

(2005, 2006) *Translated by Elżbieta Wójcik-Leese*

Marzena Broda

My Little Son Died

I must have been in need of tundra, the silence of stones,
The far off scent of the sea standing guard,
The watchful, prying eye of the fox, and the storm
Which let loose such thunder that oh!
Nothing worse could happen to us here.

I'm able to stand, move my lips, and after a while,
Mumble something that resembles a name,
Though it's hardly a word that will stretch my limbs,
Quicken my breath or clasp my fingers for minutes at a time.
When I allow myself to say it, prepared at once to pull back,
Wishing someone could do it for me,
It will breathe and breathe and breathe so long
That on its own it will press "stop." So say it.
Start to talk about my child —

No one could guess how much we worried about him.
And then, when he was four, he died.
When, it seemed to me, he was already old and wise
And raising *me.* He didn't finish what he started.
Ran off somewhere, toddling over the wood floors in bare feet,
Just a child, after all.

Remembering the details exhausts me.
I look for an excuse to rest, pull myself away,
Arrive at some other wilderness: now I see it, now I don't.
Too full of grief to let myself be caught, I push north.
There I float in streams, flow over falls,

Pool at the bottom, and plash all night
Over the oily, mackerel scales of clouds,
Which smell like little pieces of melting butter.
Right now I don't care where I am.
Someday—just have to wait long enough—I'll evaporate.

(2010, 2013)

Translated by Karen Kovacik

Joanna Lech

The Tide Coming In

Midnight, the middle of June. It's raining and Marta has finally fallen
asleep.
She sleeps with her mouth open like a fish flung onto the shore.
I watch her as the sea might.

I think she must be dreaming of the tide coming in, the saltiness of sweat.
Or maybe, as usual, she's dreaming of the dead—their clammy hands,
strange tenderness
and hunger, which makes them steal her warmth.

She doesn't complain when they visit her. She feels a little pang
and something more tart. Sometimes I think I'd like
to live in her skin, her breath,

to be the tissue of her bluish lips, when she says: I had a dream
I was a vessel, a black hole; I swallowed everything.

I feel cold, she says at daybreak.

(2008, 2008)

Translated by Karen Kovacik

Marzanna Kielar

Tide

Here neither roots nor trees can hold, neither green sheets
of saxifrage nor crusts of moss.

Only you stand fast—lofty pillars, looming bastions,
broken pulpits of basalt—cliffs in lethal conflict with the sea.

You appear immortal
as if death had died in you and through you
amid rings of surf.

As if death, ravenous as salt, did not reign,
plucking spring hatchlings from the nest:
hours when sunlight first blooms, the valley of waves swings open,
and words and fish glisten.

Death poises above its own shadow. Racing swift.
It bends, retrenches,
hits its mark. Revels in its speed.

It will carry off a house and garden pocked with thistle down, cut short
the swallow's joy of days. When death draws near, the coffee's still
steaming
and no one's brushed the crumbs from the tablecloth.

Death smears the scrim of clouds with blood, tramples the world
beneath the wheel of seasons.

Thumb circling the string
to warm up the bow—the muscles of hand and neck mute witnesses—
it swells the tide red.

(2015, 2015) *Translated by Karen Kovacik*

Julia Fiedorczuk

Bio

How unlike a dead fish a live fish is
—Maxine Hong Kingston

When I was a fish
Space had cozy walls
And as always was round

I dreamed of divine fins
Feather headdresses and life
Upon the water

It was said the tail
Drops off but there is a reward:
A pair of aching feet.

I did not believe
In fairy tales. I grew
Wings like the fronds

Of black ferns.
Where did I
Not go!

When I was a fish
There were no days,
No sex, no difference.

Warmth came
From outside. Now
In my lungs I have unbearably

Light air.
I have the lure of the sea
In my green irises.

I look at the sky: o you
Miraculous turret. I dance
For you.

(2003, 2006)

Translated by Bill Johnston

Julia Fiedorczuk

Lands and oceans

It is literally fire that is dear to us.
At times you feel it on the soles of your feet.
It's a sign that everything was once divine ocean,
while the deep time of earth is expressed in such disquieting numbers
that their discovery has changed the course of human thought.

Which, it goes without saying, expects the ground
beneath its feet, and a favorable element.
From this perspective the sun is something like eternity,
the sea a stubborn subtext.

The place
will work so long as graves can be dug.
Only in certain places can houses be built.
Despite everything there's faith in the permanence of these traces,
though everyone knows it's better to have one handful of peace.
Still other versions speak of the answered prayer of the fish.

One way or the other, chaos has its laws.
Bodies are solid, though we do have tears, and they are in every word:

for salt is on the tongue's tip and is the dot over the i.

(2005, 2006) *Translated by Bill Johnston*

III. Reimagining the Bard

In the late eighteenth century, partitioned by the empires of Austria, Russia, and Prussia, Poland disappeared from the map of Europe. Only after World War I was the Polish state finally reborn. During this long period of partition, Poland's Romantic poets—Adam Mickiewicz, Juliusz Słowacki, Zygmunt Krasiński and Cyprian Kamil Norwid—helped maintain a sense of unity and fueled the belief that literature should serve the common good. Thus, national identity and poetry became linked in the cultural imagination.

This Romantic paradigm remained relevant in Poland's political and cultural life during later periods of oppression. According to Joanna Niżyńska, the twentieth-century heirs to the Romantics regarded literature as "charged with the ethical responsibility of witnessing the community's misfortunes and working toward its survival" whether during the occupation of World War II, the communist period, or the Solidarity era. In the twentieth century, poets such as Czesław Miłosz and Zbigniew Herbert perpetuated this ethos of witness and rebellion, though Miłosz was careful to make a distinction between "the witness of poetry" and a "poetry of witness." With the imposition of Martial Law in 1981, protest poetry, published outside the censor's control, became the norm. However, even before the fall of communism in 1989, younger generations of poets criticized the kneejerk patriotism of older writers. In 1986, Piotr Sommer, editor of the journal *Literatura na świecie* [World Literature], published a special issue featuring the poetry of the New York School. He called for an "ordinary poetry" in the manner of Frank O'Hara's lunch poems to counter the "values"-laden poetry of previous generations.

This chapter shows Poland's women poets positioning themselves ironically against different aspects of this Romantic paradigm, not least the macho, insurrectionary archetype. The chapter opens with Katarzyna Boruń-Jagodzińska's "Ballad on the Death of Poet," addressed to outsider poet Kazimierz Ratoń, who died in 1983, alienated from friends, family, and the literary establishment. Boruń-Jagodzińska's poem contrasts Ratoń's solitary death with the fanfare at the deaths of great nineteenth-century men of letters who, like

Mickiewicz and Słowacki, died in exile. But the poem can also be read as a commentary on the production of literary fame and the privileges accorded the male bard.

The next two poems in this chapter reimagine Mickiewicz himself. While the historical poet left Russia for permanent exile in the West, Krystyna Lars envisions him remaining under the czar's influence and becoming a collaborator and hack. By presenting this alternative version of Mickiewicz, whose life was so central to insurrectionary Polish identity, Lars suggests the pressures to collaborate that confront any writer under a repressive regime.

Other poems assess the seemingly different literary terrain allotted men and women. Anna Piwkowska's "What Do Men Bring?" imagines male poets as dynamic, with their abacuses, laptops and Swiss watches, but also vulnerable, and in the end, the female speaker notes, not without irony: "We always survive them." In Boruń-Jagodzińska's "The Literary Life" the writerly woman appears as little more than a helpmeet or groupie—"a muse, a companion in late-night singing, a consoler of bodies" who loses her appeal as she ages—while the male poet seems a poseur who inflates his own heroics.

Szymborska's "Evaluation of an Unwritten Poem" speaks to the sometime condescending reception of women poets by critics. A pompous male reviewer deploys an arsenal of footnotes to disparage the existential and antiwar platform of the "Lady Bard"—her poetics at odds with the Romantic paradigm and her ordinary language a departure from the lofty rhetoric of rebellion and witness. The "unwritten" poem mentioned in the title could suggest that women writers have practiced self-censorship to avoid the hostile reception that sometimes awaits their work. In fact, Szymborska's poem might well be a riposte to Czesław Miłosz's patronizing description of her in *A History of Polish Literature* as a poet "who leans toward preciosity" and who "is probably at her best when her woman's sensibility outweighs her existential brand of rationalism." Of course, Szymborska, during her fifteen years on the editorial staff of the journal *Życie literackie* [Literary Life], was herself known for writing tartly ironic rejection notes, always in the first person plural, her biographers Anna Bikont and Joanna Szczęsna tell us, to disguise her gender, as she was the only woman on the staff. Thus this poem can be read in at least three ways: as a send-up of pompous, biased reviewers, an exercise in self-satire, or a gentle lampoon of some of the writers she rejected.

Joanna Mueller, Justyna Bargielska, and Marta Podgórnik also distance themselves from aspects of the Romantic paradigm while imagining an alternative literary lineage for themselves. Mueller's "Proofreading" establishes intertextual connections with Norwid, Leopold Staff (1879-1957), Tadeusz Różewicz (1921-2014) and the aforementioned poet and translator Piotr Sommer (b. 1948), longtime editor of *Literatura na świecie.* Mueller worked as a proofreader for that journal, a practice that perhaps influenced her own sound- and pun-driven poetics, full of neologisms and intentional "errors." Like many younger poets who reached adulthood after the communist era had ended, Mueller is less interested in the historical witness implied by poets like Staff, who after World War II, famously wrote, "Now when I build, I shall begin / With the smoke from the chimney." Instead she is drawn to the austere lyrics of Tadeusz Różewicz, with their embrace of the unheroic fragment. Bargielska's "Avantourism" puns on "avant-garde" and "tourism," but in Polish also contains the resonance of *awantura*, a disturbance, quarrel, or scandal. In the poem, we're confronted with two kinds of seeing: a conventional masculinist "back and forth" and another that sweeps "all around . . . in a glorious pan"—paradisiacal, exuberant, opposed to the same old tropes of rebellion. Likened to a "backhoe or peeling an apple," this sort of poetics can uproot the entire tradition from Genesis through Miłosz, aided and abetted by a cadre of female poets, represented by Joanna Mueller, to whom this poem is addressed. Podgórnik's "death becomes her" functions as a "biographia literaria" for a younger woman poet, who writes for herself rather than for "future generations" because, unlike Miłosz, she did not "survive two world wars."

The chapter concludes with two poems of praise for old women poets. Anna Kałuża has inquired why patriarchal culture allows for the mythologizing of bards without honoring the female equivalent. Filling this void are Krystyna Rodowska's poem, featuring a witchy sage who keeps a black cat inside her and can "clench enemies / with the claws of her poems," and Ewa Parma's "Old Women Poets," composed just after the death of Wisława Szymborska in 2012. Parma's poem alludes to Szymborska's final poem "Map," which appears in the last chapter of this anthology. In response to stereotypical notions of women's verse as sentimental, Parma's opens with the sentence: "They prefer maps over the truth / and the number Pi over professions of love." Both Rodowska's and Parma's poems attribute to aging women poets calm and humility in the face of bodily decline and historical tumult. Rodowska's old woman poet teaches that "rather than standing over the abyss / you nestle into it." Parma's women poets, survivors of protests and parades, manage better than their male counterparts in old age because "they're closer to the body than God." "Unwillingly," she concludes, "they become legends."

Kamila Pawluś, in an influential essay about the status of Polish women poets since the fall of communism in 1989, notes that women writers tend to be difficult to place in movements or schools and thus are often marginalized in literary criticism or anthologies. For instance, a 2011 anthology on the new Polish lyric, edited by Jerzy Borowczyk and Michał Larek, includes only one woman out of twenty-eight poets. But as we can see from the work in this chapter, these poets position themselves within and against the tradition in nuanced ways—questioning the Romantic paradigm, imagining alternative literary lineages, and polemicizing with each other.

Katarzyna Boruń-Jagodzińska

Ballad on the Death of a Poet

in memory of, among others, Kazimierz Ratoń

It used to be like this: they wait.
The surgeon tests his scalpel for sharpness—
he will cut out the heart, dispatch it
to the poet's homeland—
the urn is ready.
The sculptor sprinkles plaster
in a jar of water (still too soon—
again he'll have to throw it out).
Strange the human warmth of thickening plaster
and the stony chill of the body at rest.

It used to be like this: they wait.
The photographer with his magnesium flash
or the skillful illustrator.
The priest off in the corner or beside the bed
with God himself.
The widow checking her face in the shrouded mirror
to make sure her single tear is perfect.
The grandson playing with a cotton ball daubed in oil
touches it to the flame of a candle.

It used to be like this: they wait.
Maybe only his would-be lover
is missing,
the one who's supposed to hold his hand
until she feels the spasm

just as she had so many times in bed.
Ah, here she is, the lover,
now everyone's in place.

And him?
He's already chatting
with those on the other side.
He's humming outmoded songs,
playing the childhood game "Even and Odd"
and then "Cadavre Exquis"
because he's again in Paris.
Or he's simply settled into the bedclothes,
knowing that this long dream
will seem a mere moment.

It happened like that. It did.
Everyone's bustling around his death,
and he can't find the final line:
"There's still an hour of light
before the dark comes on,
there's still an hour of darkness
before the light. . ."
It really happened that way
some time in the past.

(1989, 1991) *Translated by Karen Kovacik*

Krystyna Lars

Soiree at the Czar's Plenipotentiary

You see his face before you, and realize you exaggerated, making of him a fiend in the grip of other devils. He is weary. The soiled cuffs of his white shirt. The dandruff on his white collar.

On the table before you, beside the champagne and pink roasted slabs of wild boar, lies the great sin of your youth: a dog-eared copy of reckless poems. They once stirred the hearts of Lithuanian students and chambermaids. Your companion smiles at you indulgently. A glass with a few drops of wine balances on the tips of his spread fingers.

You have decided to stay. The Niemen rolls undisturbed by the foot of the palace. Clover sways in the warm breeze. Cries of merchants and women hawking vegetables waft from the city. In Paris the rent for an attic apartment has gone up again, the price for anything has gone up. Nothing else is new. The same old quarrels, stupidity and filth. You look out the window. Above Castle Heights the sun with the Czar's emblem etched into its face. You have learned to hold your tongue.

You know your task is a great one, devoid of the easy pathos that attracts minds unsettled and shallow. A friend of yours just finished his epic on the planting of peas. You are at ease, confident you can write it better.

At home your shredded manuscript about an over-sensitive youth with a weakness for thunderbolts, priests and symbolic numbers. It lies in tatters on your mahogany desk. Beside it a white page and fresh-sharpened quill.

(1990, 1991) *Translated by Daniel Bourne*

Krystyna Lars

The Military Governor Contemplates the Statue of Adam M.

Buttoned waistcoat and combed hair. Not a wrinkle in his pants. His face tranquil, yet fraught with concentration, the burden of reason and responsibility. A bold gaze, but not brazen. No carved angels or classical poets. No scrolls with goose quills or unclothed symbolic ladies. Any palm leaves would be a waste of stone.

The pedestal done in good taste as well. There are ornaments, but none of them too gaudy. Flowerbeds line the wrought-iron fence. No chains to rope them off. The best touches of all are the exuberant floral arrangements hiding allusions to Crimean plant-life.

On the bronze plaque this short note: "Author of the narrative work *Comrade Thaddeus* and a verse drama in several parts, the most-noted of which describes various dreams of the author and expresses his hope for a better morrow."

Any gate in the fence would be a waste of time.

(1990, 1991)

Translated by Daniel Bourne

Katarzyna Boruń-Jagodzińska

The Literary Life

She could have been a muse,
a companion in late-night singing,
a consoler of bodies,
helpmeet in downing that last half-liter.
She could have offered triage to poets
who've not exactly died for the cause.
She could have been a wise crone,
a way-station,
a light in the window,
a Reconciliation Commission,
a designated witness,
an aide-de-memoire,
a back for slapping,
a helping hand.
She used to be.
But not any more.
She's no longer even the next scribbled number
in a string of notebooks.

So much for the literary life:
Krakowskie Przedmieście,
the basement bar of the Polish Writers' Union,
games of chess,
pierogi with potatoes and cheese,
a long sigh,
and Lou von Salomé.

(1989, 1991) *Translated by Karen Kovacik*

Anna Piwkowska

What Do Men Bring?

They bring in sand on their boots, laughter and tulips.
Abacuses, rulers, computers. Bonds and shares
from the stock exchange. Maps, the secret plans
of airports, bases, basilicas. These strategy masters
bring their compasses, Swiss watches and laptops,
leather diaries and crumpled sheets of paper,
the letters of a friend who drowned himself
from unrequited love; these utopia masters bring
their visions of marches, parades, changes of guard.
What do men bring? Pitons, crampons, poems;
they drop their faded shirts to the floor,
those which got torn under full sail and those
faded somewhere high in the white Dolomites.
We want them for the moment of a brief covenant,
when fate focuses like light in the eye's pupil.
When the point darkens, but the angle
of vision widens. Like ships in rusty docks
they're always ready to depart. Bags packed
with a tennis racket, with precious points
for matches they had won. The magnetic card
with call units, impulses under the skin, that's their asset.
We sail with them believing in fogless seas,
cicadas, almond trees, elbows tanned by the sun
—we'll pine for this moment our whole lives.
They bring washed-out books on the soul and the will
in soft, gray covers. They like heretics.
We squeeze them on the shelves among the classics
and thus our library slowly becomes complete.

Our life becomes complete. One day in fall,
together with them, we put on tar-lined coats
and kindle fires to finally expel
the plague from the city, to bury it for good.
We always survive them. Brittle light
slips with ease from the old photographs
onto our eyes and lips—like white dust, like lime.

(2002, 2004)

Translated by Elżbieta Wójcik-Leese

Wisława Szymborska

Evaluation of an Unwritten Poem

In the poem's opening words
the authoress asserts that while the Earth is small,
the sky is excessively large and
in it there are, I quote, "too many stars for our own good."

In her depiction of the sky, one detects a certain helplessness,
the authoress is lost in a terrifying expanse,
she is startled by the planets' lifelessness,
and within her mind (which can only be called imprecise)
a question soon arises:
whether we are, in the end, alone
under the sun, all suns that ever shone.

In spite of all the laws of probability!
And today's universally accepted assumptions!
In the face of the irrefutable evidence that may fall
into human hands any day now! That's poetry for you.

Meanwhile our Lady Bard returns to Earth,
a planet, so she claims, which "makes its rounds without eyewitnesses,"
the only "science fiction that our cosmos can afford."
The despair of Pascal (1623-1662, *note mine*)
is, the authoress implies, unrivaled
on any, say, Andromeda or Cassiopeia.
Our solitary existence exacerbates our sense of obligation,
and raises the inevitable question, How are we to live et cetera?
since "we can't avoid the void."
"'My God,' man calls out to Himself,

'have mercy on me, I beseech thee, show me the way...'"

The authoress is distressed by the thought of life squandered so freely,
as if our supplies were boundless.
She is likewise worried by wars, which are, in her perverse opinion,
always lost on both sides,
and by the "authoriture" (*sic!*) of some people by others.
Her moralistic intentions glimmer throughout the poem.
They might shine brighter beneath a less naïve pen.

Not under this one, alas. Her fundamentally unpersuasive thesis
(that we may well be, in the end, alone
under the sun, all suns that ever shone)
combined with her lackadaisical style (a mixture
of lofty rhetoric and ordinary speech)
forces the question: Whom might this piece convince?
The answer can only be: No one. *Q.E.D.*

Translated by Stanisław Barańczak and Clare Cavanagh

Joanna Mueller

Proofreading

> *you'll be read not to the cadence of speech*
> *but to the clang of things*
> —Piotr Sommer

The rhythm of language, the poem's rhyme
is not the rhythm of life. So here's the dilemma:
to coordinate? subordinate? agree?
Paradigms collapse, and as for syntax,
mistakes multiply: elliptical evasions,
tautological encounters. Correctness
is a matter of usage, not norm, and, in the end,
who cares? From holy Tomes, only quotes
will survive, which won't be possible
to footnote, there'll be gaps and repetitions,
sentences that spin out to infinity,
clauses that die incomplete. Blunders
occur when we wander among letters:
misplaced modifiers, a persecution complex,
a hunt for needles in haystacks.
Will shoddy forms distill anything?
People like us never build the world
with smoke from the chimney. Redaction
is reduction; the whole, a ruin, always
a fragment. We begin with phonemes. The tip
of the tongue tunnels through the gaps
between our teeth. Finally we express
the hard, voiced plosive filaments
of the Book. We gulp in order to go on,

so the proofreader who comes after us
will gallop through the pages. Manuscripts
are fragile. Though they won't burn, his
one careless move will turn them into

(2001, 2003)

Translated by Karen Kovacik

Justyna Bargielska

Avantourism

for Joanna Mueller

Tell me how I feel in this porno pop-up
near Skierniewice where I want to gaze
all around in a glorious pan
instead of the same old back and forth. I imagine
heaven will involve this kind of seeing, something like
the movements of a backhoe or peeling an apple
or an idea which yields a rain of swallows—
all of it counterclockwise.
"Back and forth" means that same guy
eating the same hot dog and reading the same old Miłosz.
I'm afraid of that hot dog since I don't know how to be the same
from one blink of the eye to the next. Blink
and the heavens will unearth me from the rain of swallows
that covered me a moment before. Maybe stand behind me
with your troops. And if I feel anything at all,
bring me word of it.

(2011, 2012)

Translated by Karen Kovacik

Marta Podgórnik

death becomes her

she decided to adopt an alternative lifestyle:
to be true to herself rather than
to future generations. she regretted
she did not survive two world wars.
she could not speak about poetry with pride.
she took pride in love, which she knew from books.
she did not wage wars or write diaries.
in a perfunctory way, she kept house,
but the jury was lenient. her bed remained empty.
someone sent her crucial instructions
and she tightened a loose screw.
she wanted to live somewhere else
but remained in her place for the greater good.
only once did she lose control
when someone in her family was insulted.
her accent left much to be desired
but sometimes flaws make a true original,
no? dramas of women gone bad
escape notice much like falling rain
when everyone sits around the bar.
in the end she got fed up with both.
she had a heart attack. literally. the doctors went overboard.
fluids trickled through her body like a sieve.
and sadly for her, she made it through.

(published 2004) *Translated by Karen Kovacik*

Krystyna Rodowska

Old Woman Poet

Apparently she's now seventy
but swift as thought
she crosses my path with the black cat
she keeps inside her
before darting into the cold

Animals have taught her
how to clench an enemy
with the claws of her poem
She's no longer
merely human

I caught sight of a willow empty-handed in winter
glowing wild in the hoarfrost

This old woman poet
shows you've got to hum
to keep from screaming

and rather than standing over the abyss
you nestle into it

(1980)

Translated by Karen Kovacik

Ewa Parma

Old women poets

prefer maps over the truth
and the number Pi over professions of love.
They roll out time like a carpet
and shake off blades of dry grass
from their first dates.
They observe parades,
processions and protests
through their curtains.
In stores, Weltschmerz
overwhelms them
among clothes racks.
At the hospital, they manage
better than male poets:
they're closer to the body than God.
With age, they smile
more frequently,
wink, make space for silence.
Unwillingly,
they become legends.

(2012, 2014)

Translated by Ewa Parma and Karen Kovacik

IV. The Ironic Art of Poetry

Edward Hirsch has noted the prevalence of the ars poetica in Poland, particularly during the communist era, "because the poets have repeatedly been called upon to justify their art." One has only to think of Czesław Miłosz's "Ars Poetica?"—its question mark suggesting a poetics based less on certainty than on mystery—or Zbigniew Herbert's "Pebble" with its praise for the stone's "ardor and coldness," its inability to be "tamed," its "calm and very clear eye," qualities the uncompromising poet cultivated in life and art. But not only historical circumstance would account for the many examples of the ars poetica by Polish women poets: surely, the wish to stake out literary ground has something to do with countering gendered expectations as well. In the 1990s, poet and critic Jerzy Jarniewicz observed that in Poland, women's poetry was still thought to be "soft," "tender, "over-emotional," "self-indulgent" and "naïve." And in 2014, Michał Larek, co-editor of a 1100-page anthology on the contemporary Polish lyric, which included only one woman, said in defense of his editorial criteria: "There's something too mild about [women's poetry], too inclined to a simple metaphysics." All of the poems in this chapter, through their ironic evocations of the art, work against such stereotypical notions of women's verse.

If poetry by women is assumed to be sentimental and sweetly drawing on natural images, many of the poets juxtapose nature and culture to ironic effect. Wisława Szymborska's "The Joy of Writing," perhaps in dialogue with Emily Dickinson's "My Life had stood—a Loaded Gun," specifically takes up issues of gender, writing, and power. Readers will recall that in Dickinson's poem, the speaker's life, the "Loaded Gun," stands dormant till possessed by the daemon, represented by the masculine "Owner." The gun and owner declare open season on the feminine, "hunt[ing] the Doe," and the gun happily gives up domestic life (sharing "the Eider-Duck's / deep pillow") in favor of laying "a Yellow Eye" or an "Emphatic Thumb" on all who would threaten it.

Szymborska's "The Joy of Writing," while also imagining a doe imperiled by hunters, changes the terms of the equation. For Dickinson, only by destroying the feminine doe could one create. But

Szymborska wittily identifies with the doe as hunter-critics surround it and prepare to attack. The poet declares her godlike power to control what happens in this textual world, which she will use not to avenge herself on the hunters but to freeze their bullets altogether. "Without my blessing," she decrees, "not a leaf will fall."

A number of other poems in this chapter also play nature off culture in their ironic versions of the ars poetica. In "The Sentence," Julia Hartwig contrasts the world of art and form with the "formlessness" of the "linden's branches unbuttoned" and the "magpie's screech." Agnieszka Kuciak, a poet known for her work in traditional forms, likens the act of writing to a memory of childhood ice-skating in the rhymed quatrains of "Hawthorn." Marzanna Kielar's "Manuscript" imagines poetry—or language itself—in an anthropological light, excavating the bogs of the Mazurian lake district, where the wind as if "voiceless . . . piece[s] together words / in a foreign tongue, feeling / for knotted nerves, hollowed syllables / under the rime." And Mira Kuś describes "a scene ripe for a lyric, the sky / dotted like a porcelain teacup"—which sounds like it could belong in a stereotypically "feminine" poem—then drops in a cat, a "bloody sparrow in his teeth."

Izabela Morska and Agnieszka Kuciak use personas to circumvent reductive, biographical interpretations of their work and to shed light on the critical reception of women poets. Morska's poetic alter ego, Madame Intuita, is the ironically named feminine counterpart of Zbigniew Herbert's Mr. Cogito. In communist Poland, Cogito was seen as an Everyman, an anarchic intellect devoted to classical literature and art, who could not be controlled by the repressive regime. But Morska's Intuita, feminist, queer and operating in a globalized world, suggests the range of gendered—and human—experience that Herbert's Cogito, from that earlier historical moment, didn't consider. Meanwhile, Agnieszka Kuciak created twenty-one poets, of whom eight are women, in her faux anthology *Distant Lands: An Anthology of Poets Who Don't Exist,* a fabulist project reminiscent of the work of Jorge Luis Borges or Fernando Pessoa. Comparing the poems to the biographical notes allows readers to see disparities between the central editor's hostile portrayal of a poet and the work itself. For example, the poet "Bionda" is condescendingly described as "a scholarship holder, a student of beauty, who tends to flit here and there." But her poem included in this chapter sounds much more commanding than the deprecating bio would indicate, ending with the lines: "a man will enter a woman through a veil / of words woven by me." Like the speaker in Szymborska's "The Joy of Writing," "Bionda" extols her ability to recreate the world.

Both Wisława Szymborska and Ewa Lipska depict poetry readings as peculiar spectacles of gendered display. In "Stage Fright," Szymborska offers a portrait of a "dowdy" poet who lacks Romantic cachet: "If only her dress were longer and more flowing / and the poems appeared not from a handbag but by sleight of hand." Lipska mocks the kinds of questions women poets might be asked at such readings: "Your favorite color? / Your happiest day? / The poem that surpassed your imagination?"

Many of the poets reject the daintiness and docility that are supposedly hallmarks of women's poetry in favor of crudeness, aggression, and power. Morska's "Madame Snake," both erotic and writerly, recalls the serpent goddesses of the ancient world, such as the Egyptian Wadjet or the Minoan Snake Goddess of Crete. Addressed to a lover, the poem speaks to an endlessly replenishing sexual power that is also spiritual and textual. Ewa Sonnenberg's "Prophecy," in a voice reminiscent of Anne Sexton's "Her Kind," depicts the poet as a kind of fated outcast "with time's fatal virus injected under her skin / a razor slash of sun on her throat." Marta Podgórnik directs her poem "little use" to a soon-to-be ex-lover: "Don't come back," she warns, "or you'll screw up / my concept for a book." And Urszula Kozioł, who has written many an ars poetica over her long career, contributes two to this chapter, including the rollicking lament "Again I Didn't Write" about the speaker's failure to produce a picaresque epic like *Don Quixote*. International in scope and intertextual in strategy, these poems about writing dismantle stereotypical notions of women's verse.

Wisława Szymborska

The Joy of Writing

Why does this written doe bound through these written woods?
For a drink of written water from a spring
whose surface will xerox her soft muzzle?
Why does she lift her head; does she hear something?
Perched on four slim legs borrowed from the truth,
she pricks up her ears beneath my fingertips.
Silence—this word also rustles across the page
and parts the boughs
that have sprouted from the word "woods."

Lying in wait, set to pounce on the blank page,
are letters up to no good,
clutches of clauses so subordinate
they'll never let her get away.

Each drop of ink contains a fair supply
of hunters, equipped with squinting eyes behind their sights,
prepared to swarm the sloping pen at any moment,
surround the doe, and slowly aim their guns.

They forget that what's here isn't life.
Other laws, black on white, obtain.
The twinkling of an eye will take as long as I say,
and will, if I wish, divide into tiny eternities,
full of bullets stopped in mid-flight.
Not a thing will ever happen unless I say so.
Without my blessing, not a leaf will fall,
not a blade of grass will bend beneath that little hoof's full stop.

Is there then a world
where I rule absolutely on fate?
A time I bind with chains of signs?
An existence become endless at my bidding?

The joy of writing.
The power of preserving.
Revenge of a mortal hand.

Translated by Stanisław Barańczak and Clare Cavanagh

Julia Hartwig

The Sentence

I believe in the sentence the pause that aims for
the grace and plainness of ordinary speech
Everything in me craves that moment when form
envelops the formlessness where I've been suspended
suffering from the mild if constant ache of the indescribable
from the scattering of my thoughts and feelings
where I live as if deprived of air
I'm not ashamed to admire the linden's branches spread wide
in the window to listen to the magpie's screech
both hectoring and blessed simply because it is
I'm not afraid to drink in the heat
of this dry and tragic summer
since the sentence the dependable sentence
helps me again feel the ground beneath my feet

(published 1987)

Translated by Karen Kovacik

Agnieszka Kuciak

Meter

At times, it's like returning home: already
on the threshold, dogs shake off whole years
of absence, and again you scratch their ears,
and at the matted table, quite unsteady,
you'll touch the dimpled wall—its penciled lore,
its map of names and dates—where years ago
you strained so tall to reach each line, to grow.
So, too, with meter, when you pause before
a wall of paper filled with dates and names,
believing in the wall, to which you'll run
from freedom's frying pan and into rhyme's
fire. But at times, like fate, it seeks to pen
intention with caesura, or run on to some other
line, one devoid of home or dogs or mothers.

(1996, 2001)

Translated by Karen Kovacik

Agnieszka Kuciak

Hawthorn

In winter, Father liked to take us here
for skating. When on frosty mornings the pond
stiffened like the Styx, we tapped a song
on the glazed water for demanding deer.

Our blades sliced the white meat
of the ice: glassy rationed slab, gristled
with light and water-veined, which whistled
and crackled under our weight.

We sped, hearts pounding, cutting the skin
of the world as if our blades' flash
had transformed that watery page through a slash
of pen into a witness's document.

Even our shadows could cut the light
(shadows like dark stigmata of shimmering things
before the zenith), where fish congeal, flung
from the water like the dead from the pit.

Then out of breath, we'd stop near the shore,
and the clouds of our breath would stall
over us, and we'd suck from the hawthorn—
our mother—snow berries, its nipples dry and cool.

(Now in summer they slip from me
like Proteus, for whom truth wouldn't last
if held long in the mouth, yet one believes
in that creed, where words have a taste;

where ice sheets keep their shape like quatrains,
and a nimble fishing-rod slips through the hole
of memory, and one's tongue gets frozen
to that world as if to a gate in the cold.)

(1994, 2001)

Translated by Karen Kovacik

Marzanna Kielar

Manuscript

autumnal peat bog—the breath of poplar and alder
shortens; light grows dwarfish, pale bonsai,
clutched in the ebb of noon;
the wind prods smoldering dry twigs,
debris of leaves trapped in a roll
of wire-netting, as if, voiceless, it pieced together words
in a foreign tongue, feeling
for knotted nerves, hollowed syllables
under the rime

(1999, 1999) *Translated by Elżbieta Wójcik-Leese*

Mira Kuś

View from My Window

As if in a Chinese miniature:
through branches of apple blossom out my window
patches of deep spring sky shone through,
dotted like a porcelain teacup
with a pattern of floating clouds.

The wind was blowing clear and light,
an image that floated yet also froze in space.

Yes, the scene was ripe for a lyric
when a cat crept into the landscape,
a bloody sparrow in his teeth.

(1978, 1988)

Translated by Karen Kovacik

Izabela Morska

Madame Intuita

My whole life's like learning a second language—
so many immigrant sacrifices but in the end
I can't get rid of this accent, recognized
everywhere to my annoyance.
And I'd been feeling almost assimilated!
All that effort, and for what?

Overwhelmed by the mystery of it,
I enroll in a class of heightened conversation.
There I also speak with an accent—
even more pronounced—and sometimes lose
whole threads or connections. It can't be helped.

You could call this a 'mother tongue'
but I don't have a mother, only a handful
of old wives' tales and myths: watch the distracted
woman dancing on a tightrope—will she fall?
will she find something to grab onto?
The careful charting of her mood swings
doesn't exactly encourage fluency.

That other language, elusive yet familiar, is like water:
slips through my fingers, empty
but for a trace of dampness, an aftertaste
of crystalline pleasure. In the meantime,
like an early Renaissance poet,
I savor the elaborate undergirding of Latin
with its praiseworthy logic.

The language of the educated classes
gives me an edge in rhetorical contests.
But in a weak moment, I neglect all
those sensible rules, and my background is suspect.
One can blot out the past with intense effort
but it will never fully disappear.

Unsure of myself, I stop speaking altogether
and just try to make out sounds—
a mountain stream spilling onto a valley of rocks
disappears like a shaky pulse, an echo,
an elf—now you hear me, now you don't—
and before I can laugh, I'm up to my knees
in layers of hurt and shame. How to wade through?

Elsewhere I come upon fragments of letters, stories broken off.
I tie up those loose ends, restore lines with my pen.
I'm content, I only look, I don't say a thing—

don't dare to breathe so as not to frighten
that roadside creature half-woman, half-beast.
When I turn around and look that way again
will I glimpse at least a print from her tiny hooves?

(2000, 2002)

Translated by Karen Kovacik

Agnieszka Kuciak

***

Sure, I'll rent out to others all my dreams,
with magnolias and a garden seen through glass,
a quail's flight erasing the tableau
where many dwelled, but never you.

My dreams feel light and clear. A table waits
with plates of cuttle-fish, where they will eat,
where a man will enter a woman through a veil
of words woven by me.

Bionda

BIONDA: A scholarship holder, a student of beauty, who tends to flit here and there. God only knows what she did in Italy—maybe she went there to daydream? She has written a number of insignificant poems—in the words of one critic: "*Dolce far niente fa pensar niente.*" She goes to the library just to describe it, and she has made numerous trips to Rome largely to parody it. Her poem "In Rome" spurred protests from a certain Catholic radio station, which called it a "great literary sin against the Holy Spirit."

(published 2005)

Translated by Karen Kovacik

Wisława Szymborska

Stage Fright

Poets and writers.
So the saying goes.
That is poets aren't writers, but who—

Poets are poetry, writers are prose—

Prose can hold anything including poetry,
but in poetry there's only room for poetry—

In keeping with the poster that announces it
with a fin-de-siècle flourish of its giant P
framed in a winged lyre's strings
I shouldn't simply walk in, I should fly—

And wouldn't I be better off barefoot
to escape the clump and squeak
of cut-rate sneakers,
a clumsy ersatz angel—

If at least the dress were longer and more flowing
and the poems appeared not from a handbag but by sleight of hand,
dressed in their Sunday best from head to toe,
with bells on, ding to dong,
ab ab ba—

On the platform lurks a little table
suggesting séances, with gilded legs,
and on the little table smokes a little candlestick—

Which means
I've got to read by candlelight
what I wrote by the light of an ordinary bulb
to the typewriter's tap tap tap—

Without worrying in advance
if it was poetry
and if so, what kind—

The kind in which prose is inappropriate
or the kind which is apropos in prose—

And what's the difference,
seen now only in half-light
against a crimson curtain's purple fringe?

Translated by Stanisław Barańczak and Clare Cavanagh

Ewa Lipska

Questions at a Poetry Reading

What's your favorite color?
Your happiest day?
The poem that surpassed your imagination?
Don't you have hope?
You're scaring us.
Why is time shot down
and the sky all black?
The empty hand, a hat floating on the sea?
Why a wedding dress
with a funeral wreath?
Hospital corridors
instead of forest paths?
Why the past and not the future?
Do you have faith? Or not?
You're scaring us.
We have to get away from you.

I try to stop them.
They fly straight into the flame.

(published 1982)

Translated by Robin Davidson and Ewa Elżbieta Nowakowska

Ewa Lipska

My Translators

My translators. They: my sequel.
My—Their—
heap of time on the table.
The thick jam of dictionaries.

A Cyrillic morning
swathed in a fog of Germanic suede.
A Romance antelope nibbles
at the edge of my poem.

My—Their—
journeys.
Paths heading *à rebours*
for no reason.

My surgeons'
transplanting of words. Them.
Untranslatable
in this brief epic.

And I
am in love with so many languages at once.
Letter by letter, I soak up the dampness in Nässjö
as I meet my bastard poems in the woods.

My—Their—
voices. This hovering over books.
Making predictions from the abyss of pages.

Syllables lifting off from Heathrow.

Will they inherit something from me?
My fear? My appetite
for endings? The plunging
necklines of meadows? Or purple fields of amethysts?

Surrounding
my—Their—
leaky reality: a paradise for hackers,
gossips and politicians.

(published 2005)

Translated by Robin Davidson and Ewa Elżbieta Nowakowska

Urszula Kozioł

To My Poem

To write a poem is like going in search of the grail
where you must depend on the enchanted comb brought by a wild boar
from the Paimpont Forest

and at times
it's like hanging on a highwire suspended from a Manhattan skyscraper
to the Eiffel Tower
dancing on that wire to spite the darkness and booming silence
beneath your feet

and sometimes
it's like picking your way through an avalanche of words
wading blindly, groping for the right one
hidden beneath heaps of silence
(where a foreigner instead of seeing a poem
perceives your odd clumps
of deaf-mute letters
as grassy runes escaped from some haystack)

or it's like
poking a twig or pen into a hive out of sheer cussedness
with no qualms about disturbing the bees
which track you
in a furious swarm
through empty fields of paper
and even drive their stingers
through the tip of your daredevil tongue

or other times
it's like hacking a quick hole
through the ice of our language
to get oxygen to the soul
starved for air in this bland expanse of days.

Oh poem of mine, let me know your name
let's get acquainted   tell me
if I have your correct address
and where I can find your hideouts.

Text me
I really want to see you
so I can make myself clear
before I leave.

(published 2010)

Translated by Karen Kovacik

Ewa Sonnenberg

Prophecy

Pour coarseness in her blood vessels
before she comes to again and sees what it's forbidden to see
Make her veins run black let her rattle them
behind the bars of withered trees scaring people away
Her punishment will be to write long poems
so long that a lifetime will not suffice
and she becomes their property
sheer as a sheet of paper
day whirling from afar into night atoning for the stars
with time's fatal virus injected under her skin
a razor slash of sun on her throat

(1998, 2000)

Translated by Karen Kovacik

Izabela Morska

Madame Snake

My forked tongue
is the root of at least
double our pleasure

Let me touch you with it
lick your body's salty tears

When I draw near, I can stroke
both of us with this tongue

I draw myself up and write
renew and return   I always get back

the sum total and more
With my slippery skin I skirt
the purest waters of excess

(2001, 2002)

Translated by Karen Kovacik

Marta Podgórnik

little use

how many brilliant phrases can i find for this sadness?
guess it depends on the form—not the poem's, but mine.
so i give in to stereotype and with a theatrical grimace
down shots leaning on the counter
just because i'm dumping you again.

but actually i'm feeling pretty sane,
and i've had it with your whole rock 'n' roll
like a firecracker up the ass, when sometimes life
should be simple, ordinary as a board game, clean as sunshine,
three frank lines that wind up in the trash.

i didn't feel like crying, i don't cry in bars,
i won't make a spectacle of our private lives.
besides, what sort of spectacle can you make
in literary magazines anyhow? unless i mentioned you
by name and wrote that you come too quick.

i won't do that. i won't even invent
some artful name for it. leave and don't come back.
i'll remain in this state of drunken nostalgia
for a few more poems. don't come back, or you'll screw up
my concept for a book.

(published 2000)

Translated by Karen Kovacik

Urszula Kozioł

Again I Didn't Write

Today I again forgot to write *Don Quixote,*
I simply cannot fathom
how I could have let this happen,

how it could have slipped my mind
that it's high time to write
my own *Don Quixote.*

It's unforgivable not to write *Don Quixote*
at least once in a lifetime.
Say what you like:
I can't wrap my mind around that.

How did this happen, somebody tell me,
that in my lifetime I completely forgot
I should write *Don Quixote.*

Laugh at me all you want
as if I'm some curious exhibit
fit for a museum of wax figures
but I get chills down my spine
when I realize I didn't manage
to write the *Quixote.*

Give me a sip of sherry
or whatever you have on hand
since I'm about to have a heart attack
when it hits me

I'll never write *Don Quixote,*
and you have no clue how much
that has always meant to me.

Stop trying to out-talk me—
and go to hell, all of you.
I can see how behind my back
you keep tapping your foreheads
though none of you little shits
can imagine what it's like when you know
you will never, ever
now write *Don Quixote.*

(published 2010)

Translated by Karen Kovacik and Ewa Hryniewicz-Yarbrough

V. A Gallery of Myths and Masks

The poems in this chapter riff on cultural stories: classical myths, fairy tales, the Old Testament, Shakespeare's *Hamlet*. They depict female characters, both villains and victims, whose stories seem ripe for reappraisal. We see women feared for their power, chastised for withholding or demanding sex, punished for defying male authority. We encounter revisions of suicidal Ophelia or Phaedra, victims of rape such as Philomela or Leda, Cassandra whose prophecies go unheeded, Lot's wife changed into a pillar of salt for turning back to look at her home. To the pre-Freudian world of myths and fairy tales, the poets add psychological depth, the discovery of motive. Like Anne Sexton or Carol Ann Duffy, they often situate archetypal characters in a contemporary context, and this shifting of the frame helps us understand the gendered predicaments of each character in a new way. Moreover, these familiar stories offer intertextual means of writing about writing, for showing female characters, often apocryphal and with minimal language, in a textual light.

This chapter opens with Agnieszka Kuciak's "Delay," which revisits a cross-dressing episode from the Achilles myth: the future warrior's mother disguises him as a girl, so he will not be called to fight in Greece's war with Troy. Odysseus, masquerading as a peddler, then tricks the boy-girl into revealing his true identity. But the poem gives agency not to Homer or the myth's characters, but to narrative itself. "The story is a woman, after all," the poem's speaker informs us. "The story must be woven. / Slowly, with a faithful hand, like a shroud." In Polish, the noun for story—*opowieść*—is feminine, and Kuciak reminds us that so many of the verbs we use for storytelling derive from needlework: weaving, spinning, stitching. The storyteller, like the three Fates, has the power to spin out a long tale or cut it short. And this chapter's poets give characters the power to shape their own narratives.

We can arrive at a new understanding of female victims and villains just by hearing stories from their points of view. "Philomela" retells the myth of the title character's rape by Tereus, her brother-in-law, who cuts out her tongue, so she cannot reveal his assault. But she is able to tell her story by weaving a tapestry. Kuciak's retelling emphasizes the obsessiveness of Philomela's craft. Like a writer who can't stop writing, Philomela is compelled to knit together cause and effect, the horrific intricacies of revenge. Two poems by Anna Piwkowska situate classical stories in a contemporary setting, also referring to tropes of weaving. "Phaedra" draws parallels between the tragic heroine, rejected in love and responsible for a lover's death, and a homeless woman who lives near a subway entrance. Like her classical counterpart, this woman also believes in a "centuries-old thread // of a story." "Ismene, sister of mine," narrated by a contemporary version of Antigone, contrasts her sister's belief in "mundanities and miracles" with her own love of "train stations and the rush of airports." Boruń-Jagodzińska's "My Name Is Iocasta" transforms the mother and wife of Oedipus, oblivious in the original, into a more urbane and ironic character, who quotes a French ballad and cracks mother-in-law jokes, noting, "A curse it is to be one's own."

This rewriting from the female character's viewpoint can present her motivation in a more complex light, as we see in the two poems by Szymborska. "Lot's Wife" gives the infamous biblical character, often compared to Eve or Pandora, the chance to explain why she turned around. And explain she does, presenting twenty-five different reasons for why she "could have" looked back. These range from rebellion ("So I wouldn't have to keep staring at the righteous nape / of my husband Lot's neck") to shame ("because we had stolen away") to physical weakness ("I felt age within me"). Taken together these many rationales complicate our understanding of the character, presenting her in a provisional, postmodern guise. "Every history we choose to tell," writes Szymborska's translator Clare Cavanagh, "is told only at the cost of countless other stories that might have been, that were but went unseen, that were seen and then forgotten or erased. Both personal narratives and grand master plots are rooted in a deeply human need to make consequence of chaos." Instead of finding only one explanation for the character's behavior—stupidity, say, or simple defiance—the multiple rationales that express "what might have been" inspire compassion rather than judgment. So, too, in Szymborska's "Soliloquy for Cassandra," we get a new insight into the prophet whose foretelling of the future was not believed: like a poet, she stands apart from those "within life," who live moment to moment instead of having the ability to take in time's epic sweep. Says Cassandra: "I loved them. / But I loved them haughtily. / From heights beyond life. / From the future." Her prophecies isolate her, and being right comes with a cost: her "city under ashes," her "head full of doubts" rather than arrogance. Szymborska inflects the stories of Lot's wife and Cassandra with the humility that comes from experiencing war and displacement firsthand.

Setting myths and tales in a contemporary context can make archetypal characters seem less remote, motivated by rage, frustration, and desire. Ewa Sonnenberg's muses in "Sign of the Times" must "sell themselves in order to live" and "have stopped believing / the words of poets"—clearly a commentary on the state of poetry in the commercialized era after communism. Krystyna Rodowska's erotic poem "Without Revenge" begins with the woman as "neither Eve triumphant / nor submissive" on her knees, working for a man's "glory." Katarzyna Ewa Zdanowicz's updated fairy tale characters—Cinderella, Red Riding Hood—also give voice to the class and gender politics of the new era. Cinderella, drunk at the ball, loses not just her slipper, but also her pants and her tights. And she lives in a passé Soviet-style apartment *blok*, which the narrator refers to ironically as her "castle of concrete." Red Riding Hood shows up in two incarnations: the young girl subjected to blame-the-victim conditioning by the culture ("don't cut through the woods / because they'll rape you / and forget to finish you off") and the vengeful vulpine figure who seizes control of her fate by killing the woodsman. In their reworking of these archetypal stories, Sonnenberg and Zdanowicz keep company with Margaret Atwood, Sylvia Plath and Anne Sexton whose "abrasive colloquialism," as Alicia Ostriker reminds us, "modernizes what is ancient and reduces the verbal glow that we are trained to associate with mythic material."

Izabela Morska's Madame Intuita poems offer a riposte to Zbigniew Herbert's Mr. Cogito series, centered around the alter ego with a Cartesian name who highlighted the absurdities of life under communism. While Mr. Cogito, a classicist, rejected the "frantic love songs" of rock and roll, "Madame Intuita, Vampire-Killer, Grants an Interview," plays with the archetype of the seductive lesbian vampire in a post-communist, media-saturated age.

The poem closing this chapter —Julia Fiedorczuk's "Madame Midas"—imagines the title character changing the things of the world not to gold as her husband did but to the "icy white" and "elegant black" of text. Instead of being frozen into hard metal, this world is constantly evolving, full of light and breath and movement.

Izabela Morska was quoted on the cover of *Madame Intuita* as saying: "I don't regard poetry as a personal voice. I'm interested in poetry as the trying on of masks." Agnieszka Kuciak initially contemplated using Rimbaud's phrase "*Je est un autre*" ["I is an other"] as the epigraph to her faux anthology of twenty-one invented poets, *Distant Lands*. The adopting of personas enables these poets to reinvent cultural stories whose archetypes have cast a long shadow.

Agnieszka Kuciak

Delay

Odysseus disguised as a peddler, Achilles disguised as a girl:
Will they recognize each other in the marketplace,
among trinkets and veils, hand-mirrors and trifles,
which the cunning Odysseus spreads out like a life?

Achilles, however, stands aloof.
The cloth's softness doesn't tempt him.
Achilles is a man, after all.
And at this market he sees only cheap fabric
and no sword.

But why does he hesitate so long
if Odysseus knows his craft
and Homer is no less adept?

Without Achilles nothing will happen.
Without Achilles the Greeks will not win.
No one will sail for Ithaca.
Without him, shrewd Odysseus will never leave.

Yet Achilles stands aloof.
In his long dress, he hesitates.
Who mandates this delay?
Who desires it, who can use it
if not the story itself?

The story is a woman, after all.
The story must be woven.

Slowly, with a faithful hand, like a shroud
long as the voyage of Odysseus.

Maybe the story hid the sword from Achilles?

(1997, 2001)

Translated by Karen Kovacik

Agnieszka Kuciak

Philomela

"If you can't speak, weave instead"—words
she managed with her tongue cut out.
And with crooked needle and dark thread,
she stitched her scream, the rapist in retreat.

There she could have stopped, but the pain returned
like Odysseus from Calypso. So she embroidered
her betrayed sister with knots of tears.

There she meant to end, but the stark stitching
led her onward. She wove her nephew's death,
and, hand shaking with fear, the banquet
where the boy was served.

She could have finished, but the stitching
went on and on, beyond myth,
outside it, covering the whole earth,
with its midden-heaps of infants, battlefields,
the ambitions of generals, your suffering
and death from a blood disease.

Philomela keeps weaving, something gives her strength,
though she will never rival a goddess.
She threads her needle, bows her head,
while above her, dangles a bird's fate.

(2000, 2001) *Translated by Karen Kovacik*

Anna Piwkowska

Phaedra

I.
They called her old, mean, sick,
half-adrift, counting on nothing.
But what is it to love a hero these days?
Maybe fools and tyrants are better.
Phaedra shaves her lovely head before the mirror,
woman, mother, pauper, beggar.
Her profile grows hard like marble
and tears set on her cheeks. Any hired mourner must feel
more than she does, they whispered in the corners.
No one tends to the garden, no one cleans the palace,
and she no longer changes her dresses, her slips.
Theseus returns, Hippolytus bows his head,
a swallow lies dead on the stones.

II.
In rainy France, Phaedra is reading a novel.
Make your way back through hexameters, hang yourself
or open your veins, she whispers to someone inside her.
She looks beyond the ring of light. In the gray shadows:
her own face, thinner, back from the dead.

III.
Old, stained brown, but no, not mad,
she talks to herself, and walks, slightly hunched,
through vast stores of samples, tubes, and testers,
lipstick dreams she places in her cart,
she mixes powders, dips her face in clay.
But her profile still looks chiseled, her name

is burned into her shoulder, bruises mark her breasts,
and on the cool stones before the subway entrance
rests her pallet, her romantic trash, her bed,
her weaving unraveled, her centuries-old thread

of a story.

(2007, 2009)

Translated by Iza Wojciechowska

Anna Piwkowska

Ismene, sister of mine

I came from the North by train,
the city familiar as the back of my hand,
everyone in the family dead. We'd waited
in vain for so many resurrections
we lost faith in returns from the underworld.

I emerged from the subway to a bright street,
trees gleamed in early green,
and hyacinths hidden all winter
peeked shyly from the ground,
purple, pink, and wet.
Our house existed, tall as a ship.
Bells were ringing, people hurried,
and on your kitchen table lay
round, smooth, lilac
eggs. Children were saying: Easter.

Where did I come from, return from, where am I from?
Back from a trip again, in a coat again, you
in a colored dress, in the kitchen as always
say to me: The Savior is risen.
You're right again, little Ismene,
You believed in mundanities and miracles,
in the glint of dishes and the smell of starch,
while I believed in train stations and the rush of airports
when I renounced you, my own.

What am I seeking, centuries later, here
in your house? The thread from the spool, pull it,
help me, because that thread is the seam of your dress.

(2007, 2009)

Translated by Iza Wojciechowska

Katarzyna Boruń-Jagodzińska

My Name Is Iocasta

The heart of a mother is alive,
so goes the French ballad,
and to this day it brings tears
to mother-in-laws' eyes.
A curse it is to be one's own,
the harshest sentence.
I'm not here, but I keep watch
so my other children
won't point out the straight and even path
to the blind one.
If only he had sinned with his eyes!
The eye of my son flew out the door
like a naughty boy,
the eye of my husband followed close behind.
Blood's voice must have summoned them,
so I hang over the crossroads
and point the way.

(1984, 1985)

Translated by Karen Kovacik

Wisława Szymborska

Soliloquy for Cassandra

Here I am, Cassandra.
And this is my city under ashes.
And these are my prophet's staff and ribbons.
And this is my head full of doubts.

It's true, I am triumphant.
My prophetic words burn like fire in the sky.
Only unacknowledged prophets
are privy to such prospects.
Only those who got off on the wrong foot,
whose predictions turned to fact so quickly—
it's as if they'd never lived.

I remember it so clearly—
how people, seeing me, would break off in midword.
Laughter died.
Lovers' hands unclasped.
Children ran to their mother.
I didn't even know their short-lived names.
And that song about a little green leaf—
no one ever finished it near me.

I loved them.
But I loved them haughtily.
From heights beyond life.
From the future. Where it's always empty
and nothing is easier than seeing death.
I'm sorry that my voice was hard.

Look down on yourselves from the stars, I cried,
look down on yourselves from the stars.
They heard me and lowered their eyes.

They lived within life.
Pierced by that great wind.
Condemned.
Trapped from birth in departing bodies.
But in them they bore a moist hope,
a flame fueled by its own flickering.
They really know what a moment means,
oh any moment, any one at all
before—

It turns out I was right.
But nothing has come of it.
And this is my robe, slightly singed.
And this is my prophet's junk.
And this is my twisted face.
A face that didn't know it could be beautiful.

Translated by Stanisław Barańczak and Clare Cavanagh

Wisława Szymborska

Lot's Wife

They say I looked back out of curiosity.
But I could have had other reasons.
I looked back mourning my silver bowl.
Carelessly, while tying my sandal strap.
So I wouldn't have to keep staring at the righteous nape
of my husband Lot's neck.
From the sudden conviction that if I dropped dead
he wouldn't so much as hesitate.
From the disobedience of the meek.
Checking for pursuers.
Struck by the silence, hoping God had changed his mind.
Our two daughters were already vanishing over the hilltop.
I felt age within me. Distance.
The futility of wandering. Torpor.
I looked back setting my bundle down.
I looked back not knowing where to set my foot.
Serpents appeared on my path,
spiders, field mice, baby vultures.
They were neither good nor evil now—every living thing
was simply creeping or hopping along in the mass panic.
I looked back in desolation.
In shame because we had stolen away.
Wanting to cry out, to go home.
Or only when a sudden gust of wind
unbound my hair and lifted up my robe.
It seemed to me they were watching from the walls of Sodom
and bursting into thunderous laughter again and again.
I looked back in anger.

To savor their terrible fate.
I looked back for all the reasons given above.
I looked back involuntarily.
It was only a rock that turned underfoot, growling at me.
It was a sudden crack that stopped me in my tracks.
A hamster on its hind paws tottered on the edge.
It was then we both glanced back.
No, no. I ran on,
I crept, I flew upward
until darkness fell from the heavens
and with it scorching gravel and dead birds.
I couldn't breathe and spun around and around.
Anyone who saw me must have thought I was dancing.
It's not inconceivable that my eyes were open.
It's possible I fell facing the city.

Translated by Stanisław Barańczak and Clare Cavanagh

Ewa Sonnenberg

Sign of the Times

Unemployed muses on the dole have stopped believing
the words of poets. They've descended from their balconies to the street,
where they sell themselves in order to live. Their stomachs, not their wings,
dictate their choices: chastity and starving to death
or a pack of chips. They've cast off their white veils and bared
their navels. This source of their inspiration, now public property,
gives rise to collective hymns.

(1994, 2000)

Translated by Karen Kovacik

Krystyna Rodowska

Without Revenge

I'm neither Eve triumphant
nor submissive
though sometimes on my knees
I work for your masculine glory
and a shot of an earthier heaven

Neither a creator avenging
that biblical rib
nor a moon: reflected
light from your life

The only thing I can do
is wrap my body
in this two-toned gown of shaky balance
(half red for desire and hurt,
the other half dark as a sky of warning stars)

my body, sisterly
and mortal

(1992)

Translated by Karen Kovacik

Katarzyna Ewa Zdanowicz

Cinderella of the Cinder-Blocks

you lost your slipper
pants and tights

you didn't notice the prince
because you were drunk

you fell asleep under the stairs
they removed your crown
sold it at a flea market
and bought champagne

tomorrow you'll wake with mildew on your tongue
and you won't feel cold or ashamed

you'll start making up a tale to tell
right after you return
to your castle of concrete

(2002, 2003)

Translated by Karen Kovacik

Katarzyna Ewa Zdanowicz

Depths

so many times they told me
—don't cut through the woods
because they'll rape you
and forget to finish you off

and you're like a twig or dry wind
a paper boat shoved in a puddle
so frail and witless that before fear kicks in
you'll actually fall for him and want to cuddle—

so I enter those woods like a watery pit
already I can't touch bottom
and the good Lord swallows me like spit

(2002, 2003)

Translated by Karen Kovacik

Katarzyna Ewa Zdanowicz

The Hunt

she wakes
amid limp wildflowers and ants parading
in a clearing beside cut trees

though the forest does not reach her heels
and her heart feels trampled
and she's dirty, snot-covered, gap-toothed and drunk
she devours a hunk of yesterday's dream, lapping it up with her lashes

in the basket there's blood
and in the blood there's laughter

grandmother had disowned Red Riding Hood,
announced a reward for anyone who'd polish her off

the woodsman had always had the hots for Red
for inside the girl lurked a wolf

(2000, 2000) *Translated by Karen Kovacik*

Izabela Morska

Madame Intuita, Vampire-Killer, Grants an Interview

No one is born
With that kind of power

To get it
You have to die a proper death
At least three times

Usually I allow them a nibble
Sometimes I have no choice
Now and then they surprise me

In those cases I lie face down
For a long time
Until I recover my reason

The miraculous effects
Of that procedure
Are also guaranteed
By our makeover salons:

"Madame Intuita & Co."
"Return to Transylvania"
And "Spectral Kiss"

Things that earlier
Might have led to your death
Now lose their power over you

But it's important to reserve
At least a quarter of your breath
For when you return

Or have someone on hand to take your pulse
And maybe thump you hard
A couple times in the chest

Sometimes it happens
You'll be gone a second too long
Too far to return

Still, there are benefits
From letting eternity's claws
Have their way with you

(2000, 2002)

Translated by Karen Kovacik

Julia Fiedorczuk

Madame Midas

changes the world into words:
icy white, elegant black.
an image stuffed into a bottle like a filigreed garden
with improbable, imitation plants.
winter clings to the soil.

the poplars, illuminated hands, shoot up to the sky.
the spirit rambles with our breath,
first in,
then out.

an awareness of light even through closed eyes.
the scrape of shovels clearing snow: in,
then out, in, then out,
in—

(2005, 2006)

Translated by Karen Kovacik

VI. Transitions, Transformations

The poems in this chapter portray girls and women at life transitions. Varied in style, they represent puberty, falling in love, childbirth, motherhood, and aging through images of disguise or dissociation, often from an oblique point of view. The characters depicted here go through bodily changes reminiscent of those in Ovid's *Metamorphoses* or the darker tales of the Brothers Grimm.

The first poem, Anna Swir's "I Banged My Head Against the Wall," revises the trope of the long-suffering Polish Mother (Matka Polka). During the time of the partitions, the Romantic poet Adam Mickiewicz envisioned Poland as the "Christ of Nations"—martyred but hoping to rise—and the Polish Mother as a sorrowful madonna, mourning the tribulations of her divided country but willing to sacrifice her sons in the struggle for freedom. As Izabela Kowalczyk has noted, the Polish Mother archetype—long-suffering, passive, sacrificing herself for her family and country—continues to have relevance in Poland. Agnieszka Mrozik has referred to this icon of traditional Polish womanhood as a "bodiless asexual madonna," her symbolic maternity more suggestive of the Marian cult than of the actual physiological processes of giving birth. In "I Banged My Head Against the Wall," Swir winks at this propensity for self-sacrifice of the Matka Polka figure while also depicting the painful realities of actual childbirth. Instead of demurely receding and giving others credit, she structures her poem as a series of boasts, using the first-person pronoun twelve times. In contrast to the Polish Mother who stayed at home while the men fought, Swir actually participated in the Warsaw Uprising of 1944, working as a nurse in an insurrectionary hospital. Some stanzas resemble the poetry of witness produced by her male counterparts: "I waited an hour / before a firing squad. / I went hungry / for six years." But to images of hunger and violence, Swir adds a brag to distinguish herself from even the most battle-hardened male soldier: "when I gave birth to a child, / they cut me open without anesthesia." In the end, the poet outdoes both Christ and nation: "Now I am resting / after three resurrections."

Krystyna Lenkowska's "An Overdue Letter to a Pimply Angel" also insists on the physiological realities of women's bodies, especially in the context of Mary's virgin birth. In fact, Lenkowska conflates the Annunciation angel, the virgin birth, and the speaker's own remembered passage through puberty. The angel atop the speaker's Christmas tree initiates the adolescent speaker into the mysteries of adult womanhood. Wearing a "white girdle," the "first / shackles of femininity," the winged emissary is said to be "hormonally sad from happiness." When the angel becomes pregnant, the fetus grows in her mouth, robbing her of speech and stretching her "bitter-salty palate into a balloon / of hopeless December hope." Only in retrospect can the speaker feel compassion for this ambivalent feminine figure.

To dramatize the changing self, many of the poets, even in short lyrics, make use of flashbacks or flashforwards. Anna Piwkowska's "Lying on a Lawn Chair" recalls a scene when the speaker, "immortal at fifteen," encountered an ill, older woman. Though the speaker's reaction at that time was "distracted, impatient, brusque," years later she remembers this meeting—particularly how the woman's smile restored color and youth to her wan face. In Julia Hartwig's "I Will Perform This Miracle for You," adult grandchildren of the poem's protagonist "hate the old age growing in her," so she tries to accommodate their denial, straightening her hunched shoulders, "her face flooded by the light of love." Agnieszka Mirahina's "To my great-great-granddaughter," composed when the poet was in her twenties, imagines a sensual connection across generations: "You'll press your ear to the earth and hear the sea / waves swelling crashing voices me / and then by and by I'll be there / licking your ear." Urszula Kozioł's speaker represents her own aging through fairy tale motifs. Like a witch, an old woman approaches her on "hunchbacked clouds," and like the heroine in a folktale, the speaker "toss[es] a mirror over [her] shoulder" to block the crone's advance. Krystyna Rodowska also dissociates the aging body from the self, likening it to a "mutinous cemetery" that has "taken [her] over, / seized everything." And the winnowing form of Krystyna Miłobędzka's "strip yourself of Krystyna" lists the self's roles—"lover tourist wife"—the poet must discard as she approaches death.

Izabela Morska's "Chrysalis" employs tropes from the life-cycle of the butterfly to suggest the fluidity of gender identity. Women "wrap themselves in tailored suits as in cocoons," the narrator tells us. Men's clothing provides a kind of camouflage for maneuvering through the patriarchy. The costume influences how the women use language and grants them access to power.

Three poems explore complexities of romantic love through animal imagery. In Agnieszka Mirahina's homoerotic "Perversion," the speaker experiments with words and images, deemed taboo by the dominant culture, to seduce her lover. Wisława Szymborska's "An Unexpected Meeting" depicts former lovers running into each other after many years. The tensions that drove them apart, now resolved, are expressed in animal terms: "Our snakes have shed their lightning / . . . . The bats flew out of our hair long ago." But the moment remains uncomfortable, for as the narrator admits, "Our humans / don't know how to talk to one another." Izabela Morska's "Metamorphoses" describes a lesbian couple's role-playing also in animal terms:

> Sometimes she's a koala
> and I a branch of eucalyptus
> Or she's a big scary King Kong
> and I her rescued innocent

As in Szymborska's poem, it is only when the speaker and her partner are being completely "human" that awkwardness ensues.

Other poems adopt some version of the male gaze to depict the self in relationship. Krystyna Miłobędzka wittily recognizes a version of her body in the statue of an archetypal goddess in Bologna, "city of botanists and philosophers." In "Over Wine," Szymborska's speaker finds herself "invented, / modeled on my own reflection / in his eyes." Being transformed by a lover's desire makes her feel "imaginary . . . so fictitious that it hurts." Drily, Szymborska's narrator places her own metamorphosis in the context of feminine origin myths authored by men: "Eve from the rib, Venus from foam, / Minerva from Jupiter's head— / all three were more real than me." And in "Blue Sweater" Anna Piwkowska elegizes a relationship via the refrain line "What will I inherit from you?" One answer is "words whispered to different women / in every tongue."

Taken together, these poems reveal a tendency to evoke life transitions in cultural terms—through allusions to classical literature and fairy tales, a fluid handling of time, a blending of the biological and anthropological, and perspectives of ironic estrangement.

Anna Swir

I Banged My Head Against the Wall

As a child
I stuck my finger in the fire
to be a saint.

As a teenager
I banged my head against a wall every day.

As a girl
I climbed from the attic window
onto the roof
in order to jump.

As a woman
I had lice.
They cracked
when I ironed my sweater.

I waited an hour
before a firing squad.
I went hungry
for six years.

Then, when I gave birth to a child,
they cut me open
without anesthesia.

Then I was killed
by lightning three times,

and I had to be resurrected three times
without anybody's help.

Now I am resting
after three resurrections.

(1978)

Translated by Piotr Florczyk

Krystyna Lenkowska

An Overdue Letter to a Pimply Angel

Do you remember the smell of sooty snow,
warmed by
the chimney?
And the taste of fir branches?
In the morning you meekly pulled
my rusty sled
to let me, the first of the first,
leave triumphant tracks
of winter in the yard.

In the evening you hung proudly
on the tree in pink
skirts of tissue paper high
and low.
I couldn't count all of you.

"Happiness," you said, "is not knowing
how much of it you have."

One winter you stole
behind the Christmas tree
in lacy hoarfrost
stockings. The white girdle, your first
shackles of femininity, wouldn't let you
rest. You stroked
your thighs under the skirt
to make them real.
You were hormonally sad from happiness.

Just like later that spring when
your first egg was fertilized
with one divine
life and grew
in your mouth.
It stretched your bitter-salty
palate into a balloon
of hopeless December hope.
You knew all its parameters.

You were still my angel.

When you fell softly and broke
into parts, I didn't hand you
a wing. Forgive me.
I too was a pimply
flightless bird.

Glory to you,
celestial bird,
from the tree
of life.

(2002, 2002) *Translated by Ewa Hryniewicz-Yarbrough*

Anna Piwkowska

Lying on a Lawn Chair

Those days were sunny and I immortal
at fifteen. I wore red shorts
and ran with the boys to catch
rust, cream and yellow butterflies
in a net. I remember the hem
of her blue linen dress,
poking out from under the wool blanket.
Beside her on the lawn a glass of tea cooled.
When we knocked it over
and said we were sorry—
distracted, impatient, brusque—
she raised her hand with difficulty
and smiled at us so brightly
that her ashen face and chest
took on color from that smile,
a girlish, golden-brown tan,
and the sun, for a moment, glistened
in the short wisps of her gray hair.
I carry that smile
like the joy of a caught yellow butterfly,
which at her request,
embarrassed, we set free.

(2008, 2010) *Translated by Karen Kovacik*

Julia Hartwig

I Will Perform This Miracle for You

dedicated to H.

They love her so much that they hate the old age growing in her. Tall and handsome, they walk by her side, and look at her with the eyes of their childhood.

Until now they hear her voice ringing in their ears like an Easter bell swinging in the friendly wind. It always accompanied her quick movements, carrying objects toward her.

So when she trips in the street, they hiss: Grandma, don't pretend!

And when she hunches over, they call: Grandma, straighten up!

Hearing it, a stranger would consider them cruel.

But once more she makes the effort, straightens up, her face flooded by the light of love.

(published 1987) *Translated by John and Bogdana Carpenter*

Agnieszka Mirahina

To my great-great-granddaughter

listen little one
I hope
some day
despite all the crackles and static you'll hear my voice
you'll press your ear to the earth and hear the sea
waves swelling crashing voices me
and then by and by I'll be there
licking your ear

(2007, 2008)

Translated by Karen Kovacik

Urszula Kozioł

***

For some time now
an old woman has been heading toward me
on hunchbacked clouds.

I toss a comb over my shoulder so the forest will block her
I toss a mirror over my shoulder so the river will stop her
but she comes ever closer
and sometimes I see her even in my dreams.

We nod at each other from afar
she looks me coolly in the eye
we're like strangers.

I still feel
the presence of a young girl inside me
(together we picked violets and marsh marigolds
and kissed a boy
on moon-splashed nights
and more than once
danced till dawn).
She's delaying her departure,
looking for excuses to live in me still—

that's why
my fingers still hold their breath in the presence of a man's fingers
and a sudden glance
sends a flutter my way.

(published 1976) *Translated by Karen Kovacik*

Krystyna Rodowska

Mutinous Cemetery

As if my body served as a bandage
—Luis Rosales

You know so little about my sovereign body:
it sleeps and bleeds and goes to work,
contains magnetic properties,
a secret pouch for hauling velvet
nine long months
which now and then will jab me
from within.

My body's highly adaptable
to whatever life brings:
making the rounds for millennia,
suited to my travels,
it lugs trunks
of threadbare feelings.

It even bears my refusal
to accept this brief span.
To distract me,
it comes down with a cough,
thinks up a "physical" pain for me,
buries the voice bestowed by love's oracle
beneath a constant rasp.

Now it has taken me over,
seized everything.

Conscientiously it warns me
it's not immortal
and I'll fare better
with other, inscrutable powers.
When the dark turns gray,
my body
becomes a mutinous cemetery.

It's still escaping
the patient sheets into live flowers.

Translated by Karen Kovacik

Krystyna Miłobędzka

***

strip yourself of Krystyna
of child mother woman
lodger lover tourist wife

what's left is undressing
trails of discarded clothes
light gestures nothing more

(2000, 2004)

Translated by Elżbieta Wójcik-Leese

Izabela Morska

Chrysalis

Lean and hungry women take on new strength
when disguised as men.
They wrap themselves in tailored shirts as in cocoons.
They savor the simplicity of the cut,
the smooth material, the presence of pockets.
Above all, they don't have to accessorize.

What's more, dressed in this manner,
they begin to speak more calmly,
with a precise elegance, no frills.
Words unspool from them,
from the core of their being,
and fitfully, they take flight.

(1999, 2002) *Translated by Karen Kovacik and Izabela Morska*

Agnieszka Mirahina

Perversion

Which word, darling, tell me which word counts as perversion?
Which word, darling, is perverse, come on, tell me which
word? Feather? cabaret? garter?
Or maybe 'woman'
but which one?
The one in the cat mask?
Or the one belling the cat?

(2007, 2008)

Translated by Karen Kovacik

Wisława Szymborska

An Unexpected Meeting

We treat each other with exceeding courtesy;
we say, it's great to see you after all these years.

Our tigers drink milk.
Our hawks tread the ground.
Our sharks have all drowned.
Our wolves yawn beyond the open cage.

Our snakes have shed their lightning,
our apes their flights of fancy,
our peacocks have renounced their plumes.
The bats flew out of our hair long ago.

We fall silent in midsentence,
all smiles, past help.
Our humans
don't know how to talk to one another.

Translated by Stanisław Barańczak and Clare Cavanagh

Izabela Morska

Metamorphoses

Hard to call it tempestuous love
when you can't stop laughing
My lover isn't a woman
She's a little critter

She has four paws and a sleek coat
We've stopped using words
Just growls and purrs
and all manner of animalness

Sometimes she's a koala
and I a branch of eucalyptus
Or she's a big scary King Kong
and I her rescued innocent
And then she's some
unidentified little ball of fur
squealing in my hands
or a wet tongue
puffing from pleasure
who sometimes to cheer me up
slides across my nose

Only as a person does
she become serious, and says:
I'm tired, I've had it
And I don't know what to turn into
how to coax her back from humanness
For a while it's all quiet

until somehow
we push past that border and
well, it's just like on the human side
here on this same old couch
feeling skittish
but it's always cozier
critter to critter

(1999, 2002)

Translated by Karen Kovacik

Krystyna Miłobędzka

***

I met myself in Bologna, city of botanists and philosophers,
I had no legs, my face was coarse and gray like a daily
newspaper, my stone breasts spurted water

this great idea I had for myself, implemented so rigorously
even the drops split and trickled back to the water

(1976, 2004)

Translated by Elżbieta Wójcik-Leese

Krystyna Dąbrowska

***

Where should I look from in order to see you?
From near or from afar? And from what point in time?
When I move away, trying to encompass you
from head to foot, like a painting on an easel,
I feel that it's you who's encompassing me,
you're changing, adding color, subtracting.
Now I'm looking you in the eyes, now I'm looking with your eyes,
while you are dreaming or as you're appearing in my dream,
and now I'm looking for a detail – an object, a gesture, a word,
may it open wide like a bud and burst into being you.
So many points of view, yet I'm stuck at a dead point,
entangled by the thread I planned to use to join them.
And I don't know if you're in the thread,
or in the flash of the scissors cutting it in two.

(2008, 2010) *Translated by Antonia Lloyd-Jones*

Wisława Szymborska

Over Wine

He glanced, gave me extra charm
and I took it as my own.
Happily I gulped a star.

I let myself be invented,
modeled on my own reflection
in his eyes. I dance, dance, dance
in the stir of sudden wings.

The chair's a chair, the wine is wine,
in a wineglass that's the wineglass
standing there by standing there.
Only I'm imaginary,
make-believe beyond belief,
so fictitious that it hurts.

And I tell him tales about
ants that die of love beneath
a dandelion's constellation.
I swear a white rose will sing
if you sprinkle it with wine.

I laugh and tilt my head
cautiously, as it to check
whether the invention works.
I dance, dance inside my stunned
skin, in his arms that create me.

Eve from the rib, Venus from foam,
Minerva from Jupiter's head—
all three were more real than me.

When he isn't looking at me,
I try to catch my reflection
on the wall. And see the nail
where a picture used to be.

Translated by Stanisław Barańczak and Clare Cavanagh

Anna Piwkowska

Blue Sweater

What will I inherit from you? Cities
with white dusks and gray dawns.
Small cafés, a street musician,
metro tickets, distant melodies.
You'd toss shillings, francs and pounds
into waiting hats. At our train station,
you'd give coins to an old woman
and scatter bread crumbs for birds.
What will I inherit from you? A fondness
for old folks. Chambray shirts,
always faded. Favorite overcoats
with missing buttons, warm
and always welcoming my arms.
What will I inherit? Your stillness
in photographs, but also gestures
and words whispered to different women
in every tongue. Maybe I'll inherit
that weakness for pretty faces,
for different skin tones or body types,
varied styles of penmanship
and unusual flavors. Blue sweater.
Scent of wet wool. Asters
on the table, shadows on the grass.
Almost impossible what we had.
Footfalls in the cathedral's long arcades.
That blue sweater will disintegrate

and not one stitch remain.
The yarn runs like snow
dissolving in the thaw.

(2002, 2004) *Translated by Karen Kovacik*

VII. The Domestic Arts

The poems in this chapter present home life and housework in a subversive light. Domestic spaces, grotesque and surreal, teem with appliances, furniture and plants that vie with humans for control. Yet the poems' protagonists often move through these dystopic settings with fortitude and wit. All seem at a remove from sentimental feminine icons such as the Romantic-era Polish Mother (Matka Polka), who places the needs of nation and family before her own; the totemic worker-mothers of socialist art, who thresh wheat and pour steel while swaddling babies; and more recently, the cheerful housewives in ads, selling everything from bottled water to dish soap.

The poets in this chapter deploy motifs of violence and estrangement to depict domestic life. Urszula Kozioł's "Recipe for the Meat Course," opens with "You need only a knife," and soon seems to be cooking up a recipe for an unsentimental poem—or a murder—with its call for Promethean fire, laurel leaves, knife, and "a compliant neck." Justyna Bargielska's "Translation" shows two generations of women on fire in a house, learning to "make room for death" while their daughters watch.

Other poems contrast the pleasures of writing with the drudgery of household work. Anna Swir's "A Woman Writer Does Laundry," compares the "healthful and useful" practice of washing clothes, a task with a clear outcome, with the "suspect" act of writing—speculative, highly impractical, but attuned to mystery. Julia Hartwig's "Escaping One's Chores" depicts fellow poets Wisława Szymborska, Urszula Kozioł and Ewa Lipska engaged in cooking, tempted by "a skinny envoy of the daemon," who lures them from their tasks to the more subversive realm of poetic inspiration. Similarly, Agnieszka Wolny-Hamkało, in "Strange Lady," shows us the writer as others see her: someone who has not yet grown up, who does not have a "normal" job, who, even after bearing children, "scribbles / letters in the sand / no one will ever read." Ewa Parma, in the ironically titled "A Room of One's Own," envies Virginia Woolf and Iris Murdoch their "afternoon meetings / with the artistic elite of Oxford and London," while her "room" is merely a deck overlooking a chestnut tree, chickens and black currant bushes.

Elsewhere the home—and even erotic life—appears mechanized, routinized or out of control. Ewa Lipska writes: "The machine of our marriage / has jammed" so "we look around nervously / for a warranty's guarantee." In one of the few poems in the chapter that focuses on a man, Katarzyna Boruń-Jagodzińska describes the "crazy" protagonist as someone who so obsessively cleans his room that the space talks back to him: "You're good, says the white wall. / You're faithful, whispers the keyhole." Agnieszka Wolny-Hamkało's "House" both surrounds and invades the woman who lives in it. The narrator lets a houseplant "lightly take root" in her and finds herself sapped of bulk and strength, but more emotionally connected to her home as a result. Izabela Morska, in "Kitchens and Myths," imagines a lesbian lover who presides over the domestic chores and also the lovemaking with the force of a giantess.

Certain images of housewives and home have the weight of myth or archetype. Agnieszka Kuciak's Mrs, K, a poetic alter ego from her faux anthology *Distant Lands,* is described as a "homegrown poet who blooms in the kitchen" and "a caretaker of her family's feelings"—a version of the Matka Polka archetype. But even as Kuciak satirizes a certain kind of religious women's verse rooted in the home, she gives Mrs. K an air of mystery and rebellion: "She who didn't want to sew her wedding gown / from a parachute will maybe someday drop down / on the far side of heaven in its pretty folds." Krystyna Miłobędzka's "The house" imagines domestic space as a tree with "lives gone into the wood." For an entire lifespan, it holds the speaker in its "interior," from the cradle to what she calls "the clearing in memory."

During the communist era, Polish poets, when writing for state publishing houses, evaded the regime's watchdogs through indirection, pitching their poems to a comprehending readership and leaving the government censors in the dark. A similar indirection operates in these poems about homes and housework, though no official censorship now exists. Written often in third person, sometimes with agency ascribed to the house or appliances, they seem directed to readers who will recognize the motifs of aggression, the notes of irony and mystery.

Urszula Kozioł

Recipe for the Meat Course

You need only a knife
and a smooth stone.
Caress the stone with the blade till the stone caresses back.
The knife should be noiseless and its sheen supple
to stiffen the resolve and steady the hand.
The rest is easy:
A stump for chopping. A pinch of salt.
Greenery for the eye to savor
and laurel leaves.
The rest is routine
because the whole art's in the seasoning.
(Don't forget the platter and colorful presentation.)
Cooking these days is no problem thanks to Prometheus
as long as there's a knife and stone.
And a compliant neck.

(published 1963)

Translated by Karen Kovacik

Justyna Bargielska

Translation

From the street, through a window, I see my mother
at the sink in a burning house, on fire herself,
so not much remains but her profile. Thirty years later,
from the street my daughter will observe me through a window
as I burn in a burning house. I don't even know
if she'll comprehend what she sees.

I've made room for death in my life,
peeled back the sheets and my shirt, unlocked my rib cage.
I wouldn't have room for any of you if I hadn't first
made space for death. As long as death didn't have a berth—
make no mistake—none of you would either.
I crack open a walnut and find the remains of a mouse
and my husband and children: my evidence, my reward.

(2009, 2009)

Translated by Karen Kovacik

Anna Swir

A Woman Writer Does Laundry

Enough typing.
Today I am doing laundry
in the old style.
I wash, I wash, rinse, wring
as did my grandmothers and great-grandmothers.
Relaxation.

Doing laundry is healthful and useful
like a washed shirt. Writing
is suspect.
Like three interrogation marks
typed on a page.

Translated by Czesław Miłosz and Leonard Nathan

Julia Hartwig

Escaping One's Chores

Dieu circule entre les pots
et les casseroles
—Teresa of Avila

Wisława's peeling potatoes
Urszula's gathering Cornelian cherries
Ewa's working at her desk on Am Gestade
St. Teresa's up to her elbows in petals
filling jars with rose-flavored jam
while a preoccupied God hovers
among pots and bowls in the convent kitchen
His face hidden beneath a brown cowl
a skinny envoy of the daemon
knocks at the convent door
and a friar working in the garden
looks up appalled from his patch of dill

(1997, 1999)

Translated by Karen Kovacik

Agnieszka Wolny-Hamkało

Strange Lady

She was supposed to grow up.
They said: maybe
after her child comes
she'll have to work
a normal job.
But no: she sits with the children
in the grass and summons ghosts
of ancient games,
and with a stick she scribbles
letters in the sand
no one will ever read.

(2006, 2007)

Translated by Karen Kovacik

Ewa Parma

A Room of One's Own

I'm sitting with Virginia and Iris,
drinking gin and tonics.
Leaves of fresh mint sail
in our glasses, and slices
of lemon swirl.
So how's it going with that room, V.?
We still miss it like hell, no?
At least there's a deck
with the morning coffee and a view
of the old chestnut tree.
All the local kids have been raised
in its shade. Now mine are.
But it's not the same
as a room with a desk,
teeming with souls of the absent greats
and the magical rustle of paper.
Yes, Iris, a person can grow stupid
from too many possessions
and dreams come true.
Piano chords from a neighbor's house
drift in as if from another planet,
and you two have no idea what it means
to fight for a scrap of time for yourself.
You with your Leonard and John
serving coffee in your stylish English homes.
Waiting for afternoon meetings
with the artistic elite
of Oxford and London.

Here conversations take place over the fence,
among the chickens and black currant
bushes, and Mrs. Dalloway,
Mme Bovary, and Mrs. Robinson
nurse their addictions
in secret. They don't shout
their wildness from the rooftops
amid mint leaves
and slices of lemon.

(2002, 2010)

Translated by Karen Kovacik

Ewa Lipska

Dishwasher

In love we're pedantic.
Dates. Times. Trained rabbits.

No problems with shedding.
Surges of idioms three times a day.

Cool drinks between twelve and two.
Newsprint detergent.
Adela with lace curtains in her rhetorical windows.

Time to start writing erotica,
you say—
marrying the dishwasher.

(published 1997)

Translated by Robin Davidson and Ewa Elżbieta Nowakowska

Ewa Lipska

Warranty

The machine of our marriage
has jammed.

We still
peel tomatoes
mince garlic
fill the evening
with talk about sex
and devour memory
after memory

yet we look around nervously
for a warranty's
guarantee.

(published 2004)

Translated by Robin Davidson and Ewa Elżbieta Nowakowska

Katarzyna Boruń-Jagodzińska

Tenant

This big guy went crazy.
He wears ribbed stockings with silver threads,
says Kiss me hard, and holds out his hand.
He has smooth skin and firm muscles.
Love knows no bounds of sex and species.
You're so soft, says the hard mattress.
You're good, says the white wall.
You're faithful, says the keyhole.
You're faithful, repeat the boxsprings.
I love your kisses, says the old teacup.
In those four walls, so many protests and innuendoes!
Faithfully the guy cleans his room.
The room rubs its dusty eyes, holds him tight,
touches his nerves, bones,
takes him in more fully than anyone.
This big guy went crazy.
And again he refuses to leave the house.

(1982, 1983)

Translated by Karen Kovacik

Agnieszka Wolny-Hamkało

The House

When she first moved in, the house
felt awkward. She was always hunting
for lost things, even a mug
was impossible to find.
They went for weeks without
seeing each other. The rooms
swallowed them up, especially the one
where she'd wake, with its black
rambling plant. Sometimes she'd lie down
among its stalks and let them grow into her,
get a little drunk, lightly take root.
She grew thin then, more pale.
But she better understood the house.
Suddenly the house allowed her
use of its cellars and lofts.

(2006, 2007)

Translated by Karen Kovacik

Izabela Morska

Kitchen and Myths

My giantess works in the kitchen
My titaness feeds me hot meals
makes sure I don't go hungry
juggles pots, twirls smoking pans

She tells me: You used to be such a skinny little chicken
and now you're my tasty little chicken morsel

She carries me to the bed and lays me out
on the sheet like a white statuette washed by waves
still sparkling from the salt and burnished by an octopus
her caresses both tender and fierce

Curled up like an oyster, I let myself be consumed
Somewhere in the background, water's running for a bath

(2000, 2002) *Translated by Karen Kovacik*

Agnieszka Kuciak

Parable

She who didn't want to sew her wedding gown
from a parachute might someday drop down
on the far side of heaven in its pretty folds.

And she who kept a key to the elevator door
for a building that no longer exists
will one day ascend to the terminal floor.

She who could tame at will
the cloud over this seething pot of potatoes—
it's as if she sat here with us still.

Mrs. K

MRS. K (PANI KRYSTYNA) is a homegrown poet who blooms in the kitchen. A caretaker of her family's feelings and the poor's, she's an exemplary wife and mother and a dedicated member of the Circle of Flying Housewives. Her poems have been broadcast on a certain Catholic station as part of the cycle "The Mysteries, Sorrowful and Joyful."

(published 2005)

Translated by Karen Kovacik

Krystyna Miłobędzka

The house

holds me in its interior   low from the roots to the darkness
of the tree   my shadow becomes its movement   its shadow
and the seasons rush headlong into the thicket.
I touch its first walls through the thickness
of years   through lives gone into the bark   between cradle
and doors the tide cut deeply into hard wood.
On the edge   from the quiver it has one entrance only
high up flame tears along the skin towards the whirr
in the windlass of green   until the arms creak.
Where will it touch the meadow   the clearing in memory?

(1965, 1970)

Translated by Elżbieta Wójcik-Leese

VIII. Curating Objects

Ordinary objects played a starring role in twentieth-century literature and art. In that century of revolutions, scientific and political, common things offered familiarity and safety, a refuge from the manipulations of ideology. As Zbigniew Herbert once observed, "Language is an impure tool of expression. It is tortured, banalized, subjected to shabby tricks . . . Therefore, the poet's dream is to reach to the words' pristine sense, to give the proper word to things." From William Carlos Williams' "The Red Wheelbarrow" to Pablo Neruda *Odas elementales* to Francis Ponge's *Le parti pris des choses* (often translated into English as *The Voice of Things*), from Duchamp's "readymades" to Joseph Cornell's "assemblages," poets and artists have used objects as touchstones of history and culture; emblems of identity or interiority; icons of familial affiliation; and markers of thresholds between body and psyche, past and future. In this chapter, we see the poets putting ordinary objects to all of these uses.

Given Poland's volatile history during the last century, it's not surprising that common objects—a map, a glove—would accrue cultural and historical significance. During periods of peace and prosperity, it's possible to take ordinary things for granted; not so, after war, or even after 1989, when the country's borders opened, travel became freer, and globalized consumer goods flooded the once empty shops. Julia Fiedorczuk's "Drawer" celebrates a catch-all space that holds "shavings of the past": magazines "containing all the beauty of the world," fabric scraps "used to make gowns for every occasion," "a map of an obsolete world." Her poem can be read as an ars poetica: like the drawer, poetry collects and preserves traces of the past, and the fact that generations of poets before Fiedorczuk claimed to "write for the drawer," to eschew publication in venues censored by the state, lends the drawer the resonance of a personal archive with broader cultural meaning. Wisława Szymborska's "Map," thought to be the last poem she wrote, riffs on the ways maps alter "objective" reality. "More delicate than the historians' are the mapmakers' colors," observed Elizabeth Bishop, a poet Szymborska admired. "Map" alludes to the conventions of cartography: colors that represent hills and forests, black dots to indicate population density, and dotted lines marking the borders of countries, which the poet describes as "barely visible / as if they wavered: to be or not." These representational practices simplify and soften the truth. "Mass graves and sudden ruins," Szymborska notes drily, "are out of the picture." She admits she likes maps "because they lie" in presenting fixed versions of cities, countries, or continents, removed from the flux of history.

Two poems by Julia Hartwig imbue this notion of an archive with an existential resonance. "Justly" begins with the proposition that every item in it "costs five zlotys" (between two and three dollars at the current exchange rate): "an umbrella and a diamond tiepin / . . . a rara avis and a canary in a cage / an antique book and a laundry bill." Time causes the value of disparate items to level, so "everything costs the same." Hartwig's "Inventory," like "Justly," opens with the idea of objects losing value over the course of a long life "like after a post-season sale": "light dresses since summer's over / winter furs autumn capes / rubber boots after the rain has passed / foreign banknotes removed from circulation." But by the end of the poem, this catalogue of cast-off items, "this heap of memories," is something the speaker, to avoid detection, must consign to "the fire's prying eye."

Objects bought, used, or worn can also represent the tastes and personality of a consumer. Walter Benjamin, writing about the nineteenth-century shopping arcades of Paris, saw them as "a world in miniature" where "the commodity intermingles and interbreeds as images in the most tangled of dreams." Rather like a globalized twenty-first century arcade, Ewa Sonnenberg's "Love Poem" assembles goods from a united Europe, likening a lover to the "warmest radiator," the "priciest bottle of perfume on the Champs-Élysées," and musical compositions such as "Schubert's 'Unfinished' and Beethoven's 'Fate.'"

Objects can also trace complex familial relations, as we see in poems by Joanna Wajs and Ewa Chruściel. Wajs describes a childhood "glove," embroidered with suns by the mother later in life, leaving the adult daughter with no "right to enter into the covenant /

between [her] mother and the girl / [she] once was." Chruściel's "Ginkgo Leaves" shows the mother, "an entrapped ghost" whose "head is full of yellow secrets," and the daughter, stooping on a Manhattan street to pick up these tiny "oars." They are linked by the fan-shaped leaves, despite their differences. And Chruściel's "Incense" makes a metaphorical connection between the beekeeper's smoker, an implement that coaxes the insects back to their hives after a swarm, and a religious ritual. Wielding the smoker, her father becomes a "priest" to the bees, who "bow to him, trembling" like "oracles."

Ordinary things evoke thresholds between wildness and domestication, childhood and maturity, reality and imagination, life and death, body and spirit. Marzanna Kielar's sound-drenched poem extols the ability of portraiture and still life to freeze time. Krystyna Miłobędzka's poem about brooches, like a Zen koan, recalls the plants, animals, and minerals that gave rise to the jewels pinned to a collar. Mira Kuś employs the metaphor of a paraffin lamp to summon the lost world of a rural childhood. Joanna Wajs reimagines the "botanical kingdom" under a table, full of mystery and surprise, from the perspective of a child. Joanna Mueller's "Etch A Sketch," shaped like a skull and crossbones, centered on the page as it might on the screen of the children's toy, offers an elegy for the child-self whose past will disappear with a "jiggle" of the wrists as she acquires the trappings of adult self-consciousness. Ewa Lipska's "A Door Handle," perhaps written in conversation with Francis Ponge's "The Pleasures of the Door," depicts the handle as a guardian of discretion, rather "like a young / Greta Garbo," that most enigmatic of actresses. Wisława Szymborska's "Negative" likens the light-on-dark world of a film strip to the ghostly appearance of the dead among the living.

Can objects have a gender outside of grammar, where in Polish, "moon" and "flower" are masculine nouns? Many of the poems in this chapter subtly suggest feminized traces of existence—through images of drawers, maps, gowns, capes, boots, jewelry, gloves, magazines, and mutable leaves—to construct an archive of being, intimate as a glove and emblematic as a map.

Julia Fiedorczuk

Drawer

Some collect shavings of the past.
They're as precious as hoarfrost on roadside birches—
especially valuable at the rare moments of absolute presence of mind,
of equinox.

Its keepsakes: piles of illustrated magazines containing all the beauty in
the world.
Scraps from fabric that was used to make gowns for every occasion.
Colored yarns. A cushion. Beneath all this
someone will one day discover a map of an obsolete world—
a landscape of defunct countries.
Herds of long-dead animals feeding on an extinct species of grass.
Houses eroded by water and by wind, and in the houses
faded photographs of those who once lived there.

(2005, 2006)

Translated by Bill Johnston

Wisława Szymborska

Map

Flat as the table
it's placed on.
Nothing moves beneath it
and it seeks no outlet.
Above—my human breath
creates no stirring air
and leaves its total surface
undisturbed.

Its plains, valleys are always green,
uplands, mountains are yellow and brown,
while seas, oceans remain a kindly blue
beside the tattered shores.

Everything here is small, near, accessible.
I can press volcanoes with my fingertip,
stroke the poles without thick mittens.
I can with a single glance
encompass every desert
with the river lying just beside it.

A few trees stand for ancient forests,
you couldn't lose your way among them.

In the east and west,
above and below the equator—
quiet like pins dropping,
and in every black pinprick

people keep on living.
Mass graves and sudden ruins
are out of the picture.

Nations' borders are barely visible
as if they wavered—to be or not.

I like maps because they lie.
Because they give no access to the vicious truth.
Because great-heartedly, good-naturedly,
they spread before me a world
not of this world.

Translated by Claire Cavanagh

Julia Hartwig

Justly

Everything costs five zlotys
Every object on this table
costs five zlotys
neither more nor less

an umbrella and a diamond tiepin
a platter and a metal buckle
a rara avis and a canary in a cage
an antique book and a laundry bill
an oar and a telephone receiver
Nikifor's paints and the comb of Violetta Villas

You can put on this table
any object you want
a notary's act and a leaflet
a violin and a pact with the devil
everything costs the same
Who would want to waste time calculating the price

(published 2007)

Translated by John and Bogdana Carpenter

Julia Hartwig

Inventory

And everything loses value like at a post-season sale
light dresses since summer's over
winter furs autumn capes
rubber boots after the rain has passed
foreign banknotes removed from circulation
telegrams—I'm coming!—in which the heart beats fast
and those the postman delivers with alarm
newspaper clippings you don't understand
letters not fit to be left behind for anyone
these troubling remainders this heap of mementos
awaiting the fire's prying eye

(1997, 1998)

Translated by Karen Kovacik

Ewa Sonnenberg

Love Poem

You're the prettiest fridge where I toss
my berries, peaches, beans and peas
You're the worst-cut jacket
in this country bought for a song
You're Hewlett-Packard's newest laser printer
reaming out scandalous excerpts of the lives of would-be mystics
You're the warmest radiator on every floor of this world
You're the priciest bottle of perfume on the Champs-Élysées
You're high-fidelity Technics equipment reproducing
Schubert's "Unfinished" and Beethoven's "Fate"
You're the longest rainbow in the sky over Paris
You're the Concorde departing with unearthly haste
You're the toughest seed in Burgundy's juicy pulp
You're a demographic peak on a cosmic scale
You're the most beautiful doorknob in this city
You're all the kings and queens at once
You're the unplayed chess match in the world championships
You're the disconcerted piano in the psychiatrist's salon
You're the showiest shop window in central London
You're the swankest hotel entrance in the Hilton chain
You're the glossiest page of *Vogue*
You're the priceless dessert fork at the dinner party
You're the most compelling table of contents lent for minutes at a time
You're the best injection against rabies and the flu
You're grave as the Tower of London
You're sweet as a heap of sugar cubes
You're grand as the tallest skyscraper in New York

(1999, 2001)

Translated by Karen Kovacik

Joanna Wajs

glove

a woman in a red jacket
picked up a glove from the snow
—smaller than a sparrow on an ice-covered branch—
and carefully hung it on a tree

a few days later
in my mother's cupboard
I found gloves with woolen suns—
a ray climbing up each finger

I shuddered to think
she embroidered them herself
I was unsure if they'd been mine
and she
had slipped them off my hands
wrapped them in a scarf
and tucked them in the highest cupboard
jealous of my gaze like a squirrel
who won't hide a nut
while you watch

I was a bit surprised
she carried them as if they were her aggrieved children
and I, her adult daughter, stood in the door
with no right to enter into the covenant

between mother and the girl
I once was

suddenly I felt I cast no shadow

(2004, 2004) *Translated by Karen Kovacik*

Ewa Chruściel

Ginkgo Leaves

Your mother gave you a ginkgo leaf before she died,
thousand-year inhabitant of the Permian ocean growing
inside us as we study the blueprints of waiting

My mother, too, is an entrapped ghost

Her veins of thoughts collide in cacophonies
Her head is full of yellow secrets

These leaves push me forward
as I walk the Manhattan streets to meet her
I kneel and pick them—they become oars—

My mother stoops in the park to collect
the same leaves

In multitudes we can only give
what we received

these groves inside us

(2008, 2011)

This poem was composed in English.

Ewa Chruściel

Incense

My dad's
a master beekeeper.
For the bees he's a veritable
cosmonaut, his smoker
an accordion from a different planet
or a tin bird with a knapsack.

Or he's a priest
and the smoker his incense.

The drunken bees like oracles
bow to him, trembling.

(2006, 2009)

Translated by Karen Kovacik

Marzanna Kielar

***

Hand that sketches me now while I look at the neck
of a guinea hen—her long, thin quills lanced
with streaky white. Their glossy blue-black tips.
The silky crest atop her crown.
Her back speckled like black enamel.

Hand that sketches the strawberry's striated pulp,
denser beneath the skin, juice ruddy on the tongue,
the hum of bees in its leaves—

not a trace will remain,
though your unwavering line brings order to this tumult.
And filling in each surface
sharpens that vision.

Against whose death did you stream in this light among the stones
in the rough gravel of hours?

(2005, 2006) *Translated by Karen Kovacik*

Krystyna Miłobędzka

****

Brooches once lived in the wild. They slept underground, swung on branches, ran through the woods, poured down tree bark. When resin clotted into amber, when pomegranate grains hardened enough for polishing, when tusks fell from the elephants, and seeds from pinecones gave way to forest after forest—only then were the brooches domesticated with pin and clasp.

(1961, 1962)

Translated by Karen Kovacik

Mira Kuś

From the Land of Childhood

Tiny village in a valley
on three sides bordered by woods
and the fourth by an absent road
In winter it drifted over with snow
in spring and fall
mud cut if off from the world
That tiny point
invisible on maps
is like a paraffin lamp
held aloft
scattering the dark
Whoever swings it
sends me a sign

(2009, 2010)

Translated by Karen Kovacik

Joanna Wajs

under the table

in the kingdom under the table two gold masks gleam:
the moon and the lamp with their open mouths

you crawled under when a crayon fell and every night since you drift off
in this botanical kingdom among the peat animals

during dinner you spy on the grownups' knees
they call to you in the ringing of flatware you hear the laughter of roots

(2010, 2010) *Translated by Karen Kovacik*

Joanna Mueller

Etch A Sketch

some day I'll surrender
to adulthood's stranglehold
and no one then will wish me well
and none among the living will be loving
I'll jiggle the past with my wrists hurl blame
scam search engines edit exploits into boilerplate
even as I'm etherized with everyone's needs
and the child I've ceased to be nods off in me
and all instincts of teeth and tongue atrophy
your demands will accompany my decline
there'll be less and less of me for me
I'll become common shallow
unseizable in sorrow
called to be obsolete
but hear me out

until
that day
arrives

I won't take it and I won't quit

[auto-epitaph]

(2008, 2010)

Translated by Karen Kovacik

Ewa Lipska

A Door Handle

In the sun's brass
it looks like a young
Greta Garbo.

It contains
the travel itinerary
of our hands.

Discreet,
it closes the door
on our studies' whispers.

During
family quarrels
it slams the voices shut.

Gilded with ambition
it has its style.

Sometimes it falls.
Like deafening silence.

It despises
the rusty padlock,
confidant of our
sinful thoughts.

At the sight of it
it spits out the key.

(published 2007)

Translated by Robin Davidson and Ewa Elżbieta Nowakowska

Wisława Szymborska

Negative

Against a grayish sky
a grayer cloud
rimmed black by the sun.

On the left, that is, the right,
a white cherry branch with black blossoms.

Light shadows on your dark face.
You'd just taken a seat at the table
and put your hands, gone gray, upon it.

You look like a ghost
who's trying to summon up the living.

(And since I still number among them,
I should appear to him and tap:
good night, that is, good morning,
farewell, that is, hello.
And not grudge questions to any of his answers
concerning life,
that storm before the calm.)

Translated by Stanisław Barańczak and Clare Cavanagh

Works Cited

Note: All quotations from Polish-language texts are translated by Karen Kovacik unless otherwise indicated.

Alexievich, Svetlana. *War's Unwomanly Face*. Moscow: Progress Publishers, 1988. Print.

Barańczak, Stanisław. *A Fugitive from Utopia: The Poetry of Zbigniew Herbert*. Cambridge, Mass. and London: Harvard UP, 1987. Print.

Benjamin, Walter. "Dream Kitsch: Gloss on Surrealism." *Selected Writings: 1927-1934*. Vol. 2. Ed. Michael Jennings. Cambridge, MA: Belknap Press of Harvard UP, 1999. Print.

Bikont, Anna and Joanna Szczęsna. *Pamiątkowe rupiecie. Biografia Wisławy Szymborskiej*. Kraków, Znak: 2012. Print.

Boland, Eavan. *Object Lessons: The Life of the Woman and the Poet in Our Time*. New York and London: Norton, 1995. Print.

Cavanagh, Clare. *Lyric Poetry and Modern Politics: Russia, Poland, and the West*. New Haven and London: Yale UP, 2009. Print.

Chowaniec, Urszula, Kirsi Kukijärvi, and Marja Rytkönen. "Mapping Concepts: 'Experience' and Women's Writing in Russia and Poland." *Mapping Experience in Polish and Russian Women's Writing*. Ed. Marja Rytkönen et al. Newcastle Upon Tyne, UK: Cambridge Scholars Publishing, 2010. 1-29. Print.

Cyranowicz, Maria, Joanna Mueller and Justyna Radczyńska. *Solistki: Antologia poezji kobiet (1989-2009)*. Warszawa: Staromiejski Dom Kultury, 2009. Print.

Fiedorczuk, Julia. "A gdzie poetki?" [Where are the women poets?] *Gazeta Wyborcza* 28 Mar. 2014. Web. 22 June 2014.

Grzegorzewska, Wioletta and Marek Kazmierski. "A Transformation in Verse: Reconnaissance of Developments in Polish Poetry Since 1989." *Polish Literature in Transformation*. Ed. Ursula Phillips. Berlin: Lit Verlag, 2013. 251-264. Print.

Gutorow, Jacek. *Niepodległość glosu. Szkice o polskiej poezji po 1968 roku*. Kraków: Znak, 2003. Print.

Herbert, Zbigniew. "Pebble." Trans. Czesław Miłosz. *Zbigniew Herbert: Poezje wybrane / Selected Poems*. Warszawa: Wydawnictwo Literackie, 2000. 39. Print.

Hirsch, Edward. *How to Read a Poem and Fall in Love with Poetry*. New York, San Diego, London: Harcourt Brace, 1999. Print.

Hirsch, Marianne. *Family Frames: Photography, Narrative and Postmemory*. Cambridge, MA and London: Harvard University Press, 1997. Print.

Hoffman, Krzysztof. "Nic się nie stało. Druga część rozmowy z Jerzym Borowczykiem i Michałem Larkiem." *e-czas kultury.pl*. Jan. 24, 2014 (178). Web. 23 June 2014.

Janion, Maria. "Rozstać się z Polska." *Gazeta Wyborcza* 20 Oct. 2004: 14-16. Print.

Janion, Maria. *Życie pośmiertne Konrada Wallenroda*. [The Posthumous Life of Konrad Wallenrod.] Warszawa: PIW, 1990. Print.

Jarniewicz, Jerzy. "Poland, Poetry, and Gender." *Women's Studies International Forum* 18.1 (1995): 45-50. Print.

Kałuża, Anna. "Poezja kobieca." *Edupedia.pl*. Web. 24 August 2012.

Kowalczyk, Izabela. *Matki Polki, Chłopcy i Cyborgi. . . Sztuka i feminizm w Polsce*. Poznań: Galeria Miejska "Arsenał," 2010. Print.

Lusty, Natalya and Helen Groth. *Dreams and Modernity: A Cultural History*. London: Routledge, 2013. Print.

Miłosz, Czesław, ed. *The History of Polish Literature*. 2nd ed. Berkeley, Los Angeles and London: U of California P, 1983. Print.

Miłosz, Czesław. *The Witness of Poetry*. Cambridge, Mass. and London: Harvard UP, 1983. Print.

Mrozik, Agnieszka. "Motherhood as a Source of Suffering: On the Contemporary Polish Discourse of Maternity." *Mapping Experience in Polish and Russian Women's Writing*. Ed. Marja Rytkönen, Kirsi Kurkijärvi, Urszula Chowaniec, and Ursula Phillips. Newcastle Upon Tyne: Cambridge Scholars Publishing, 2010. 214-239. Print.

Niżyńska, Joanna. "The Impossibility of Shrugging One's Shoulders: O'Harists, O'Hara, and Post-1989 Polish Poetry." *Slavic Review* 66.3 (Fall 2007): 463-483. Print.

Ostriker, Alicia. "The Thieves of Language: Women Poets and Revisionist Mythmaking." *Coming to Light*. Ed. Diane Wood Middlebrook and Marilyn Yalom. Ann Arbor: U of Michigan P, 1993. 10-36. Print.

Paloff, Benjamin. "Cure for the Common Cold War: Postwar Polish Poetry." *The Nation* (29 Jul. 2009). Web. 7 Mar. 2015.

Pawluś, Kamila. "Lista (nie)obecności i sztuka uważnego czytania. Poezja tworzona przez kobiety po roku 1989." *Raport: Kongres Kobiet Polski*. Warszawa: Fundacja Feminoteka, 2009.135-148. Print.

Phillips, Ursula. "Introduction." *Polish Literature in Transformation*. Berlin: Lit Verlag, 2013. 3-24. Print.

"Poland: Domestic Violence Law Debated." *New York Times* (6 Feb. 2015). Web. 16 Mar. 2015.

Rascaroli, Laura. "Like a Dream: A Critical History of the Oneiric Metaphor in Film Theory." *Kinema: A Journal for Film and Audiovisual Media* (Fall 2002). Web. 22 Jul. 2014.

Sasinowski, Alan. "Rozmowa z Katarzyną Ewą Zdanowicz, autorką tomu poezji *Ciemność Resort SPA*." *Gryfia Nagroda Literacka dla Autorki Szczecin*

2014. nagrodagryfia.pl. Web. 19 Jul. 2014.
Staff, Leopold. "Foundations." Trans. Czesław Miłosz and Leonard Nathan. *A Book of Luminous Things: An International Anthology of Poetry*. Ed. Czesław Miłosz. San Diego, New York, London: Harcourt Brace, 1996. 295. Print.
Szymborska, Wisława. "Notes from a Nonexistent Himalayan Expedition." *Poems: New and Collected, 1957-1997*. Trans. Stanisław Barańczak and Clare Cavanagh. New York, San Diego and London: Harcourt, Brace, 1998. 18-19. Print.
Śliwiński, Piotr. *Przygody z wolnością: uwagi o poezji współczesnej*. Kraków: Znak: 2002. Print.
Wachtel, Andrew Baruch. *Remaining Relevant after Communism: The Role of the Writer in Eastern Europe*. Chicago and London: U of Chicago P, 2006. Print.
Zechenter, Katarzyna. "Motherhood and the Transmission of Memory in Texts by Polish-Jewish Writers." *Polish Literature in Transformation*. Ed Ursula Phillips. Berlin: Lit Verlag, 2013. 155-174. Print.

Works Consulted

Barańczak, Stanisław and Clare Cavanagh, ed. and trans. *Spoiling Cannibals' Fun: Polish Poetry of the Last Two Decades of Communist Rule.* Evanston: Northwestern University Press, 1991. Print.

Blacker, Uilleam. "Polish Urban Literature and the Memory of Lost Others." *Polish Literature in Transformation*. Ed. Ursula Phillips. Berlin: Lit Verlag, 2013. 35-50. Print.

Borowczyk, Jerzy and Michał Larek, eds. *Powiedzieć to inaczej. Nowoczesna polska liryka*. Poznań: WBPiCAK, 2011. Print.

Carpenter, Bogdana. *The Poetic Avant-Garde in Poland, 1918-1939*. Seattle and London: University of Washington Press, 1983. Print.

Centrum Badania Opinii Społecznej. *O roli kobiet w rodzinie.* Warsaw: Fundacja Centrum Badania Opinii Społecznej, 2013. Print.

Davis, Shannon N. and Theodore N. Greenstein. "Cross-National Variations in the Division of Household Labor." *Journal of Marriage and Family* 66 (December 2004): 1260-1271. Print.

Dehnel, Jacek, ed. *Six Polish Poets*. Todmorden, UK: Arc Publications, 2008. Print.

Drugie europejskie badania jakości życia: Życie rodzinne i praca. Luksemburg: Urząd Publikacji Unii Europejskiej, 2010. Print.

Dunin, Kinga. *Czytając Polskę*. Warszawa: Wydawnictwo W.A.B., 2004. Print.

Dziewanowska, Małgorzata, Viktoriya Khomuk, and Liat Krawczyk. "Airing the Dirty Laundry: Exploring the Challenges of Domestic Violence in Poland." *Humanity in Action*. n.d. Web. 16 Mar. 2015.

Frąckowiak-Sochańska, Monika and Sabina Królikowska, eds. *Kobiety w polskiej transformacji, 1989-2009: Podsumowania, interpretacje, prognozy.* Toruń: Wydawnictwo Adam Marzałek, 2010. Print.

Graff, Agnieszka. "The Land of Real Men and Women: Gender and E.U. Accession in Three Polish Weeklies." *The Journal of International Institute* 15.1 (Fall 2007). Web. 6 Mar. 2015.

Graff, Agnieszka. *Rykoszetem: Rzecz o płci, seksualności i narodzie.* Warszawa: Wydawnictwo W.A.B., 2008.

Grol, Regina, ed. Ambers Aglow: *An Anthology of Contemporary Polish Women's Poetry, 1981-1995*. Houston: Host Publications, 1996. Print.

Honet, Roman, ed. *Poeci na nowy wiek.* Wrocław: Biuro Literackie, 2010. Print.

Hryciuk, Renata E. and Elżbieta Korolczuk, eds. *Pożegnanie z Matką Polką? Dyskursy, praktyki i reprezentacje macierzyństwa we współczesnej Polsce*. Warszawa: Wydawnictwo Uniwersytetu Warszawskiego, 2012. Print.

Jung, Dawid and Marek Kazmierski, eds. *Free Over Blood.* London: Off Press, 2011. Print.

Kałuża, Anna. "Stracone złudzenia." *Tygodnik Powszechny* (8 Dec. 2009). Web. 21 Feb. 2015.

Martin, W. "Introduction, New Polish Writing." *Chicago Review* 46.3 & 4 (2000): 7-9. Print.

Miłosz, Czesław, ed. *Postwar Polish Poetry.* 3rd, expanded ed. Berkeley and Los Angeles: University of California Press, 1983. Print.

Nowakowska, Urszula and Emilia Piwnik. "Kobiety w rodzinie." Trans. Urszula Nowakowska. *Kobiety w Polsce,* 2003. Warszawa: Centrum Praw Kobiet, 2003. 49-90. Print.

Rich, Adrienne. "Vesuvius at Home: The Power of Emily Dickinson." *On Lies, Secrets, and Silence.* New York: Norton, 1979. 157-183. Print.

Stala, Marian. *Niepojęte: jest. Urywki nie napisanej książki o poezji i krytyce.* Wrocław: Biuro Literackie, 2011. Print.

Warkocki, Błażej. *Homo niewiadomo: polska proza wobec odmienności.* Warszawa: Wydawnictwo Sic!, 2007. Print.

Wójcik-Leese, Elżbieta. "Rewritten Presences: Anthologies of Polish Poetry in English, 1989-2011." *Polish Literature in Transformation.* Ed. Ursula Phillips. Berlin: Lit Verlag, 2013. 265-280. Print.

Zembrzuszka, Agnieszka. "The Socialist Model of Woman in Poland and Its Soviet Prototype." *Topics in Feminism, History and Philosophy.* Vol. 6. Ed. Dorothy Rogers, Joshua Wheeler, Marina Zavacká, and Shawna Casebier. Vienna: IWM, 2000. 1-10. Print.

PRIMARY SOURCES (POLISH)

Note: This bibliography contains only materials from which poems for the anthology were translated. The editor also consulted other works by the poets before making her final selections.

Bargielska, Justyna. *Bach for my Baby.* Wrocław: Biuro Literackie, 2012. Print.

Bargielska, Justyna. *China Shipping.* Kielce: kserokopia.art.pl, 2005. Web.

Bargielska, Justyna. *Dating Sessions.* Kraków: Zielona Sowa, 2003. Print.

Bargielska, Justyna. *Dwa fiaty.* Poznań: WBPiCAK, 2009. Print.

Boruń-Jagodzińska, Katarzyna. *Muzeum automatów.* Bydgoszcz: Pomorze, 1985. Print.

Boruń-Jagodzińska, Katarzyna. *Więcej.* Warszawa: Staromiejski Dom Kultury, 1991. Print.

Broda, Marzena. *Zwykłe rzeczy.* Warszawa: Wydawnictwo Nisza, 2013. Print.

Chruściel, Ewa. *Sopiłki.* Toronto and Rzeszów: Polski Fundusz Wydawniczy w Kanadzie, 2009. Print.

Dąbrowska, Krystyna. *Białe krzesła.* Poznań: WBPiCAK, 2014. Print.

Dąbrowska, Krystyna. *Biuro podróży.* Kraków: Zielona Sowa, 2006. Print.

Fiedorczuk, Julia. *Planeta rzeczy zagubionych.* Wrocław: Biuro Literackie, 2006. Print.

Fiedorczuk, Julia. *Tlen.* Wrocław: Biuro Literackie, 2009. Print.

Filipiak [Morska], Izabela. *Madame Intuita.* Warszawa: Nowy Świat, 2002. Print.

Hartwig, Julia. *Wiersze wybrane.* Kraków: Wydawnictwo a5, 2010. Print.

Keff, Bożena. *Utwór o Matce i Ojczyźnie.* Kraków: ha!art, 2008. Print.

Kielar, Marzanna Bogumiła. *Brzeg: Wybór wierszy.* Warszawa: Oficyna Wydawnicza Łośgraf, 2010. Print.

Kozioł, Urszula. *Horrendum.* Kraków: Wydawnictwo Literackie, 2010. Print.

Kozioł, Urszula. *Wybór wierszy.* Warszawa: Czytelnik, 1976. Print.

Kozioł, Urszula. *Żalnik.* Kraków: Wydawnictwo Literackie, 1989. Print.

Kuciak, Agnieszka. *Dalekie kraje: antologia poetów nieistniejących.* Kraków: Znak, 2005. Print.

Kuciak, Agnieszka. *Retardacja.* Kraków: Zielona Sowa, 2001. Print.

Kuś, Mira. *Zioła i amaranty: wybór wierszy.* Kraków: Księgarnia Akademicka, 2012. Print.

Lars, Krystyna. "Ci, którzy przychodzą w snach." *Odra* (Jan. 1987): 66-67. Print.

Lars, Krystyna. *Umieranki i inne wiersze.* Gdańsk: Tytuł, 1989. Print.

Lech, Joanna. *Zapaść.* Print. Łódź: Stowarzyszenie Polskich Pisarzy Oddział w Łodzi, 2009. Print.

Lipska, Ewa. *Gdzie indziej.* Kraków: Wydawnictwo Literackie, 2005. Print.

Lipska, Ewa. *Miasteczko Świat.* Kraków: Wydawnictwo Literackie, 2007. Print.

Lipska, Ewa. *Utwory wybrane.* Kraków: Wydawnictwo Literackie, 1986. Print.

Miłobędzka, Krystyna. *zbierane*. Wrocław: Biuro Literackie, 2006. Print.
Miłobędzka, Krystyna. *zbierane, gubione: 1960-2010*. Wrocław: Biuro Literackie, 2010. Print.
Mirahina, Agnieszka. *Radiowidmo*. Wrocław: Biuro Literackie, 2009. Print.
Mueller, Joanna. "Korekta." *Poeci na nowy wiek*. Ed. Roman Honet. Wrocław: Biuro Literackie, 2009. 179-180. Print.
Mueller, Joanna. *Wylinki*. Wrocław: Biuro Literackie, 2010. Print.
Parma, Ewa. *W strefie ognia*. Nowa Ruda: Mamiko, 2010. Print.
Piwkowska, Anna. *Farbiarka*. Kraków: Znak, 2009. Print.
Piwkowska, Anna. *Lustrzanka*. Warszawa: Zeszyty Literackie, 2012. Print.
Piwkowska, Anna. *Niebieski sweter*. Warszawa: Wydawnictwo Nowy Świat, 2004. Print.
Podgórnik, Marta. *Pięć opakowań: 1993-2008*. Wrocław: Biuro Literackie, 2010. Print.
Rodowska, Krystyna. *Wiersze przesiane*. Rzeszów: Podkarpacki Instytut Książki i Marketingu, 2012. Print.
Sonnenberg, Ewa. *Smycz*. Wrocław: Wydawnictwo Astrum, 2000. Print.
Szymborska, Wisława. *Wiersze wybrane*. Kraków: Wydawnictwo a5, 2010. Print.
Szymborska, Wisława. *Wystarczy*. Kraków: Wydawnictwo a5, 2011. Print.
Wajs, Joanna. *sprzedawcy kieszonkowych lusterek*. Kraków: Zielona Sowa, 2004. Print.
Wolny-Hamkało, Agnieszka. *Nikon i Leica*. Poznań: Wojewódzka Biblioteka Publiczna i Centrum Animacji Kultury, 2010. Print.
Wolny-Hamkało, Agnieszka. *Spamy miłosne*. Kraków: Wydawnictwo a5, 2007. Print.
Zdanowicz, Katarzyna Ewa. *Deadline*. Katowice: Stowarzyszenie Inicjatyw Wydawniczych w Katowicach, 2007. Print.

Primary Sources (Bilingual and English-Language Editions)

Boruń-Jagodzińska, Katarzyna. "My Name Is Iocasta." Trans. Karen Kovacik. *Rowboat: Poetry in Translation* 1 (Spring 2011): 35. Print.

Boruń-Jagodzińska, Katarzyna. "The Literary Life." Trans. Karen Kovacik. *Private* 41 (Summer 2008): 57. Print.

Fiedorczuk, Julia. "Bio," "Drawer," "Lands and oceans." Trans. Bill Johnston. *World Literature Today* (Nov.-Dec. 2014): 30-32. Print.

Filipiak [Morska], Izabela. "Domestic Myths," "Madame Intuita." Trans. Karen Kovacik. *Kritya: A Journal of Poetry* [India] (May 2009) 4.12. Web. 14 Aug. 2014.

Filipiak [Morska], Izabela. "Mme. Intuita, Vampire-Killer, Grants an Interview." Trans. Karen Kovacik. *What I Want from You: Voices of East Bay Lesbian Poets.* Eds. Linda Zeiser and Trena Machado. Pittsburg, CA: Raw Art Press, 2006. 57-58. Print.

Grzegorzewska, Wioletta. *Pamięć Smeny / Smena's Memory.* Trans. Marek Kazmierski. London: Off Press, 2011. Print.

Hartwig, Julia. *In Praise of the Unfinished: Selected Poems*. Trans. John and Bogdana Carpenter. New York: Knopf, 2008. Print.

Hartwig, Julia. *It Will Return*. Trans. John and Bogdana Carpenter. Evanston, IL: Northwestern University Press, 2010. Print.

Kielar, Marzanna Bogumiła. *Salt Monody.* Trans. Elżbieta Wójcik-Leese. Brookline, MA: Zephyr, 2006. Print.

Kuciak, Agnieszka. "Delay," "Philomela" [two poems and an introduction]. Trans. Karen Kovacik. *Southern Review* 48.2 (Spring 2012): 312-317. Print.

Kuciak, Agnieszka. *Distant Lands: An Anthology of Poets Who Don't Exist.* Trans. Karen Kovacik. Buffalo, NY: White Pine Press, 2013. Print.

Kuciak, Agnieszka. "Meter," "Wroniecka [Street Pool]." Trans. Karen Kovacik. *Six Polish Poets*. Ed. Jacek Dehnel. Todmorden, UK: Arc, 2008. 121, 123, 125. Print.

Kuś, Mira. "From the Land of Childhood." Trans. Karen Kovacik. *Southern Review* 46.4 (Fall 2010): 643. Print.

Kuś, Mira. "Poem of the Seven Veils." Trans. Karen Kovacik. *Mid-American Review* (2011): 143-165. Print.

Lech, Joanna. "Cuts," "Postscript," "The Tide Coming In." Trans. Karen Kovacik. *Rowboat* 5 (Spring 2013): 41, 43, 45. Print.

Lenkowska, Krystyna. *Zaległy list do pryszczatego anioła / An Overdue Letter to a Pimply Angel.* Trans. Ewa Hryniewicz-Yarbrough. Rzeszów: Mitel, 2014. Print.

Lipska, Ewa. *The New Century*. Trans. Robin Davidson and Ewa Elżbieta

Nowakowska. Evanston, IL: Northwestern University Press, 2009. Print.
Miłobędzka, Krystyna. *Nothing More / Więcej nic*. Trans. Elżbieta Wójcik-Leese. Introduction by Robert Minhinnick. Todmorden, UK: Arc Publications, 2013. Print.
Parma, Ewa. "Coal Miner's Daughter: An Interview with Ewa Parma" [including Karen Kovacik's translation of her poem "A Room of One's Own" and co-translation with Parma of "Old Women Poets"]. *World Literature Today* (Nov. 2013): 40-42. Print.
Piwkowska, Anna. "Ismene, sister of mine." Trans. Iza Wojciechowska. *Inventory* (October 2011) 2: 36-37. Print.
Piwkowska, Anna. "Phaedra." Trans. Iza Wojciechowska. *eXchanges* (Winter 2012). Web.
Piwkowska, Anna. "What Do Men Bring?" Trans. Elżbieta Wójcik-Leese. *Six Polish Poets*. Ed. Jacek Dehnel. Todmorden, UK: Arc, 2008. 35, 37. Print.
Sonnenberg, Ewa. "Sign of the Times." Trans. Karen Kovacik. *With Our Eyes Wide Open: Poems of the New American Century*. Ed. Douglas Valentine. Albuquerque: West End Press, 2014. 27. Print.
Swir, Anna. *Talking to My Body*. Trans. Czesław Miłosz and Leonard Nathan. Port Townsend, WA: Copper Canyon. 1996. Print.
Szymborska, Wisława. *Here*. Trans. Clare Cavanagh and Stanisław Barańczak. New York: Houghton Mifflin, 2010. Print.
Szymborska, Wisława. *Map: Collected and Last Poems*. Trans. Clare Cavanaugh and Stanisław Baraczak. Boston: Houghton Mifflin Harcourt, 2015. Print.
Szymborska, Wisława. *View with a Grain of Sand*. Trans. Stanisław Barańczak and Clare Cavanagh. San Diego, New York, and London: Harcourt Brace, 1993. Print.
Świrszczyńska, Anna. *Building the Barricades*. Trans. Piotr Florczyk. Seattle: Calypso Editions, 2011. Print.

Notes on the Poets

Justyna Bargielska (b. 1977) is the author of the collections *Nudelman* (2014), *Bach for My Baby* (2012), *Dwa fiaty* [Two Fiats] (2009), *China Shipping* (2005), and *Dating Sessions* (2003). Her work has received numerous awards, including the Rilke Prize in 2001 and the Literary Prize of Gdynia in 2010. Bargielska's poetry has been included in many anthologies and has been translated into English, Bulgarian and Slovenian. She lives in Warsaw.

Katarzyna Boruń-Jagodzińska (b. 1956) is the author of *Mały Happening* [A Little Happening] (1979), *Muzeum automatów* [Museum of the Machines], 1986, and *Więcej* [More] (1991). A volume of her poems *Pocket Apocalypse*, translated by Gerry Murphy, appeared in Ireland in 2006. Boruń-Jagodzińska attended the Iowa International Writing Workshop in 1988 and is an active member of the Association of Polish Writers. She lives in Warsaw.

Marzena Broda (b. 1965) was born in Kraków and currently lives in a village in southern Poland, in view of the Beskid Mountains. She's the author of four collections of poetry, most recently *Zwykłe rzeczy* [Ordinary Things], 2013, two novels, and the play *Skaza* [Flaw], which was produced for Polish television. She has taught creative writing in the gender studies program at Jagiellonian University. Her poetry has been translated into many languages.

Ewa Chruściel (b. 1972) is Associate Professor of English at Colby-Sawyer College in New Hampshire, where she teaches creative writing and world literature. She's the author of two collections of poems in Polish, and *Strata* and *The Contraband of Hoopoe in English.* With Miłosz Biedrzycki, she translated a selection of Jorie Graham's poetry into Polish (Biuro Literackie, 2013).

Krystyna Dąbrowska (b. 1979) studied graphic art at the Academy of Fine Arts in Warsaw. She translates poetry from English, including W.C. Williams, W.B. Yeats, Thomas Hardy, Charles Simic, and Ruth Padel. She has published three collections of poetry, *Czas i przesłona* [Time and Aperture], *Biuro podróży* [Travel Agency] and *Białe krzesła* [White Chairs]. The latter received two major awards—the Szymborska Prize and the Kościelski Prize—in 2013.

Julia Fiedorczuk (b. 1975) is the author of five collections of poetry, a novel, and a collection of short stories, all from Biuro Literackie. Fiedorczuk teaches at the University of Warsaw and is a member of the Association for the Study of Literature and the Environment.

Wioletta Grzegorzewska [pseudonym Wioletta Greg] (b. 1974) has published poems in the anthologies *Solistki* and *Free Over Blood*. The author of six collections of poetry, she issued the bilingual *Pamięc Smieny / Smena's Memory* (2011) and *Orinoko* (2008). In 2006, she emigrated to England and currently lives in Ryde on the Isle of Wight. Her *Finite Formulae and Theories of Chance* (Arc Publications, 2014), published under the name Wioletta Greg and translated by Marek Kazmierski, was shortlisted for the 2015 Griffin Prize.

Julia Hartwig (b. 1921) was born in Lublin and studied Polish and Romance languages in secret meetings of Warsaw University and the Catholic University of Lublin during World War II. After the war she held a fellowship to Paris, funded by the French government. During the 1970s, she participated in the International Writing Program at the University of Iowa and lectured at several North American universities. The author of many collections of poetry, she has also translated into Polish a number of French and American poets, including Guillaume Apollinaire, Blaise Cendrars, Allen Ginsberg, Marianne Moore, Pierre Reverdy and William Carlos Williams. Two collections of her work, translated by John and Bogdana Carpenter, have appeared recently in English: *In Praise of the Unfinished: New and Selected Poems* (Knopf, 2008) and *It Will Return* (Northwestern, 2009). In 2014, she won the prestigious Szymborska Prize for her collection *Zapisane* [Having Been Written]. She lives in Warsaw.

Bożena Keff (b. 1948) is a poet, critic, and essayist. She has conducted literary research at the Jewish Historical Institute in Warsaw and teaches gender studies at Warsaw University and elsewhere. Her books include *Utwór o Matce i Ojczyźnie* [The Thing About Mother and Fatherland], *Barykady. Kroniki obsesyjne* [Barricades. Obsessive Chronicles], *Postać z cieniem. Portrety Żydówek w polskiej literaturze od końca XIX wieku do 1939 roku* [Character with a shadow. Portraits of Jewish women in Polish literature from the late 19th century through 1939], and *Antysemityzm. Historia niezamknięta* [Antisemitism. History Without End].

Marzanna Kielar (b. 1963), recipient of numerous prestigious Polish and European prizes for her work, is the author of five collections of poetry. Her work has been translated into twenty-three languages and has appeared in nearly forty anthologies. *Salt Monody,* a collection of Kielar's work brought into English by Elżbieta Wójcik-Leese, was published by Zephyr Press in 2006. She has held fellowships to the University of Iowa's International Writers Workshop, the Baltic Centre for Writers and Translators, among other literary centers in Asia and Europe. A member of Poland's PEN Club and the Association of Polish Writers, she lives in Warsaw and Brussels. Kielar teaches at the Maria Grzegorzewska University.

Urszula Kozioł (b. 1931) studied Polish literature at the University of Wrocław.

She's associated with the "Generation of '56," a group of writers, which included Miron Białoszewski, Jerzy Harasymowicz, Marek Hłasko, and Edward Stachura, who also debuted in that year, a time of relative openness after the death of Stalin. Since 1972, she has edited the highly regarded literary journal *Odra*. She won the Kościelski Foundation Prize in 1946, the Literary Prize of the Polish PEN-Club in 1998, and numerous other national and international awards for her work. The author of eighteen collections of poetry—most recently *Klangor* (2014), nominated for the prestigious Nike Prize—she lives in Wrocław.

Agnieszka Kuciak (b.1970) is the author of two collections of poetry, *Retardacja* [Delay] and *Dalekie kraje: antologia poetów nieistniejących* [Distant Lands: An Anthology of Poets Who Don't Exist]. The latter appeared in Karen Kovacik's translation from White Pine Press in 2013. Kuciak is also an esteemed translator of Italian literature, who brought Dante's *Divine Comedy,* the sonnets of Petrarch, and Umberto Eco's *History of Beauty* into Polish. She lives in Poznań.

Mira Kuś (b. 1948), born in Gorlice, studied physics at Jagiellonian University. She's the author of seven collections of poetry, most recently *Zioła i amaranty* [Herbs and Amaranths] in 2011. A longstanding member of the Association of Polish Writers, she has participated in numerous cultural exchanges, and her work has been translated into English, German, Russian, Spanish and other languages. A chapbook of her poems, *Beneath an Avalanche of Waking*, appeared in *Mid-American Review* in 2011. She lives in Krakow.

Krystyna Lars (b. 1950) is the author of numerous collections of poetry, most recently *Zaprosimy do nieba cały świat* [We invite the entire world to heaven] (2014), and editor-in-chief of Tytuł Press. A longtime member of the Polish PEN Club and the Association of Polish Writers, Lars lives and works in Gdańsk.

Joanna Lech (b. 1984), originally from Rzeszów, lives and works in Krakow. The author of three collections of poetry, most recently *Nic z tego / Nothing of This* (Off Press, 2011), she has been the recipient of a number of literary prizes, including the 2007 Rilke Award in the sixth All-Poland Poetry Competition, held in the city of Sopot. Her work has appeared in recent anthologies from Off Press and Biuro Literackie.

Krystyna Lenkowska (b. 1957), poet and translator, lives in Rzeszów. She's the author of eight collections of poetry, and her work in Ewa Hryniewicz-Yarbrough's translation has appeared in a number of North American literary journals, including *Boulevard, Chelsea,* and *Confrontation*. Her poetry has also been translated into Czech, Slovak, Serbian, Italian and French. She's a member of the Association of Polish Writers.

Ewa Lipska (b. 1945), with her first collection in 1967, became associated became associated with the Polish New Wave [Nowa Fala], along with poets Adam Zagajewski and Stanisław Barańczak. The author of twenty-seven volumes of poetry, Lipska has received numerous awards, including the Robert Graves PEN-Club Award for lifetime achievement in poetry. From 1991-97, she worked for the Polish embassy in Vienna, directing the Polish Institute. A selection of her work, *The New Century,* translated by Robin Davidson and Ewa Elżbieta Nowakowska, appeared from Northwestern in 2009.

Krystyna Miłobędzka (b. 1932) is the author of numerous collections of poetry. Her work has been been recognized with many awards, including the Minister of Culture Prize (2001), the Fourth Column Literary Award for her life's work (2004), and Wrocław's Sibelius Poetry Prize (2009). She has also written many scripts for children's theatrical productions. She lives in Puszczykowo, near the city of Poznań. A bilingual collection of her work, *Nothing More / Więcej nic* (2013) appeared from Arc Publications (Todmorden, U.K.) in Elżbieta Wójcik-Leese's translation.

Agnieszka Mirahina (b. 1985) is the author of three collections of poetry, and her poems have appeared in *Poeci na nowy wiek* [Poets for the new century], an anthology of younger Polish poets, published in 2010 by Biuro Literackie. She lives and works in Warsaw.

Izabela (Filipiak) Morska (b.1961) authored the collection of poems, *Madame Intuita* (2002), as well as numerous works of prose and the full-length drama *Księga Em* [The Book of M], based on the life of the transgender writer Maria Komornicka. From 2003-2006, she held a visiting position at the University of California Berkeley, and she currently teaches American literature and culture at the University of Gdańsk.

Joanna Mueller (b. 1979) is associated with the neo-Language poetry movement in Poland. With several other poets, she signed the Neo-Language Manifesto (2002), which called for greater attention to the importance of sound play in poetry and to the visual shape of the text on the page. Together with Maria Cyranowicz and Justyna Radczyńska, she edited *Solistki,* an anthology of younger Polish women poets. The author of four collections of poetry, most recently *intima thule,* she lives in Warsaw with her large family, where she helps lead a seminar on women's literature called "A Common Room," a play on the Polish translation of Woolf's "A Room of One's Own.

Ewa Parma (b. 1961) is a poet and translator of British and American poetry. She's the author of four collections of poetry, most recently *Kobiety i ważki* [Women and Dragonflies]. Her poems have appeared in English translation in the

Los Angeles Review, Mr. Cogito, Artful Dodge, International Poetry Review, and *World Literature Today*. She lives in Katowice.

Anna Piwkowska (b.1963), known for her work with traditional rhyme and meter, is the author of nine collections of poetry. A member of the Polish Writers' Association, she has received the Georg Trakl Prize and a Kościelski Foundation Distinction, and in 2014, her young adult novel *Franciszek* was awarded the Warsaw Literary Prize. An expert on the Russian Acmeist poets, she also authored a book about Anna Akhmatova. A selection of her work was published in *Six Polish Poets* (Arc Publications, 2008). Her niece Iza Wojciechowska is translating Piwkowska's *Farbiarka* [The Dye-Girl]. She lives in Warsaw.

Marta Podgórnik (b. 1979) is the author of nine collections of poetry, including *Zawsze* [Always] and *Nic o mnie nie wiesz* [You know nothing about me]. Recipient of the prestigious Gdynia Literary Prize, she works as editor for Biuro Literackie in Wrocław and is active as a literary critic and translator. She has brought into Polish the work of Auden, Lovelace, Roethke, Ciaran Carson, and Tom Waits, among others.

Krystyna Rodowska (b. 1937), originally from Lvov, studied the philology of Romance languages at Warsaw University, and is an acclaimed translator of Jorge Luis Borges, Octavio Paz, Francisco García Lorca, Gabriel García Márquez, Pablo Neruda, Vicente Aleixandre, Paul Éluard, Jules Laforgue, and Andre Breton. A generous selection of her own poetry appeared in 2011. She received the ZAiKS Authors' Association Prize for her distinguished achievements in the translation of French and Spanish-language writers.

Ewa Sonnenberg (b. 1967) is the author of nine collections of poetry, including *Płonący tramwaj* [Burning Tram] and *Smycz* [Leash], as well as her *Collected Poems* (2015). Her collection *Hazard* won the Georg Trakl Prize. Her work has been translated into many languages and has appeared in numerous international anthologies. Sonnenberg lives and works in Kraków.

Wisława Szymborska (1923-2012) was awarded the 1996 Nobel Prize in Literature. Sometimes described as the "Mozart of Polish poetry," she was praised by the Nobel committee for her "ironic precision." In 1953, she joined the editorial staff of the journal *Życie literackie* [Literary Life], where she continued to work until 1981. For many years, she wrote a book review column for that journal under the heading "Non-required Reading." Though earlier in her career she belonged to the dominant Polish United Workers' Party, she later became quietly involved in the opposition, publishing in the underground journal *Arka* and in *Na Głos* [Out Loud], the spoken magazine performed monthly in Krakow under the direction of poet Bronisław Maj. Szymborska was also a translator of French literature, particularly Baroque poetry, into Polish. She died at her home in Krakow in 2012.

Anna Swir (Świrszczyńska) (1909-1984), born in Warsaw, was the daughter of an artist. During World War II, she joined the Polish resistance and worked as a nurse during the Warsaw Uprising. Her wartime experiences made their way into her poetry, most notably in *Building the Barricade*, issued in a recent translation by Piotr Florczyk (Calypso Editions, 2011). Czesław Miłosz and Leonard Nathan also produced translations of her work in English, *Talking to My Body* (1996) and *Happy as a Dog's Tail* (1985).

Joanna Wajs (b. 1979) is managing editor of the press Nasza Księgarnia [Our Bookstore]. Her first collection *Sprzedawcy kieszonkowych lusterek* [Pocket Mirror Salesmen] won several awards, including the prestigious Iłłakowiczówna Prize in Poland. She also translates Italian literature, including the work of Umberto Eco, Italo Calvino, and Tiziano Terzani. Her translation of Vanni Bianconi's poems is a finalist in the 2016 European Poet of Freedom contest. In 2006-2011, she wrote a regular poetry column in Poland's daily newspaper, *Gazeta Wyborcza.*

Agnieszka Wolny-Hamkało (b. 1979) is the author of eight collections of poetry. She works closely with *Gazeta Wyborcza,* Polish Radio, and the television station TVP Kultura, where from 2009-2011, she ran the program Wholesale Books. Creator of performance art, she has displayed work in the Łódź gallery Manhattan and the Wrocław gallery Entropy.

Katarzyna Ewa Zdanowicz (b. 1979) is a poet, journalist and translator. The author of seven collections of poetry, most recently *Ciemność Resort Spa* [Darkness Resort Spa] (2013), she also produced a scholarly monograph on the transgender writer Maria Komornicka, *Kto się boi Marii K? Sztuka i wykluczenie* [Who's Afraid of Maria K? Art and Exclusion].

Notes on the Translators

Stanisław Barańczak was a poet, translator, editor, and literary critic. Author of thirteen collections of poetry and numerous volumes of literary criticism, he was one of Poland's most distinguished translators both from English into Polish (Shakespeare, Auden, Dickinson, Donne, Frost, and many others) and Polish into English. With Clare Cavanagh, he won the PEN Translation Prize in 1996 for their translation of Wisława Szymborska's *View with a Grain of Sand.* Professor of Slavic Languages and Literatures at Harvard University, he died in 2014.

Daniel Bourne, Professor of English at the College of Wooster, is the author of two volumes of poetry, most recently *Where No One Spoke the Language* (Custom Words Press, 2006) and the translation of Tomasz Jastrun's political poetry *On the Crossroads of Asia and Europe* (Salmon Run, 1998). His translations have appeared widely in such journals as *Field, Salmagundi, Virginia Quarterly Review,* and others.

Bogdana Carpenter, Professor Emerita of Slavic Languages and Literatures and of Comparative Literature at the University of Michigan, is the author of *The Poetic Avant-Garde in Poland, 1918-1939*, and *Monumenta Polonica: The First Four Centuries of Polish Poetry,* as well as other works. With John Carpenter, she has produced many translations of Polish poetry.

John Carpenter, a poet and literary critic, is the author of *Creating the World* and a study of the literature of the Second World War. Among the translations John and Bogdana Carpenter have done as a team are seven volumes of poetry by Zbigniew Herbert and Julia Hartwig's *In Praise of the Unfinished* (Knopf, 2008) and *It Will Return* (Northwestern, 2010).

Clare Cavanagh is Professor of Slavic and Comparative Literary Studies Chair of the Department of Slavic Languages and Literatures at Northwestern University. Her book *Lyric Poetry and Modern Politics: Russia, Poland, and the West* (Yale, 2010) received the 2010 National Book Critics Circle Award in Criticism. She has translated the work of Adam Zagajewski and Wislawa Szymborska, for which she received, with Stanisław Barańczak, the PEN Prize for Outstanding Translation. Her most recent volume, with Stanisław Barańczak, is Wisława Szymborska's *Map: Collected and Last Poems* (Houghton Mifflin Harcourt, 2015).

Robin Davidson is a poet, translator, and professor of literature and creative writing at the University of Houston, Downtown. In 2003-4 she served as Fulbright professor of American literature at the Jagiellonian University in Kraków, Poland.

With Ewa Elżbieta Nowakowska, she translated Ewa Lipska's *The New Century* (Northwestern, 2009), and serves on the editorial board of Calypso Editions. In 2015, she was named Houston Poet Laureate.

Piotr Florczyk is a poet, essayist, and translator of six volumes of Polish poetry, including *The Folding Star and Other Poems* by Jacek Gutorow (BOA Editions, 2012), *Building the Barricade and Other Poems of Anna Swir* (Calypso Editions, 2011), and *Been and Gone: Poems of Julian Kornhauser* (Marick Press, 2009). His most recent books are *Barefoot,* a chapbook of poems, and *Los Angeles Sketchbook*, a volume of brief essays, photographs, and a poem.

Ewa Hryniewicz-Yarbrough is an essayist and translator of poetry, including Janusz Szuber's *They Carry a Promise* (Knopf, 2009). Her essays have appeared in *Threepenny Review, TriQuarterly,* and *American Scholar.* She has also translated a volume of selected poems of Philip Levine into Polish (Znak, 2013) and edited a Polish collection of Ruth Padel's poetry (Znak, 2015).

Bill Johnston is a prolific translator of Polish literature. His version of Wiesław Myśliwski's *Stone Upon Stone* (Archipelago, 2010) won the 2012 PEN Translation Prize and the National Translation Award in 2012. He has also translated Tomasz Różycki's *Twelve Stations,* Magdalena Tulli's *In Red,* and Tadeusz Różewicz's *New Poems*, winner of the Found in Translation Award. Professor of Comparative Literature at Indiana University, he was awarded the Transatlantyk Prize by the Polish Book Institute in 2014 for his outstanding promotion of Polish literature abroad.

Marek Kazmierski, a writer and translator, lives in Warsaw. He is the founder of Off Press, which recently published an anthology of younger Polish poets called *Free Over Blood.* His nonfiction won a Penguin Decibel Prize. His translation of Grzegorzewska's *Finite Formulae and Theories of Chance* was shortlisted for the 2015 Griffin Prize.

Karen Kovacik received a 2011 NEA Fellowship in Literary Translation and a 2004-5 Fulbright Research Grant to Poland. Her translation of Agnieszka Kuciak's *Distant Lands: An Anthology of Poets Who Don't Exist* appeared from White Pine Press in 2013, longlisted for the National Translation Award in 2014. Professor of English at Indiana University-Purdue University Indianapolis, she's the author of the poetry collections *Beyond the Velvet Curtain* and *Metropolis Burning.*

Antonia Lloyd-Jones, a full-time translator of Polish literature, is twice winner of the Found in Translation award. She has translated works by several of Poland's leading contemporary novelists, including Paweł Huelle and Jacek Dehnel, and the authors of reportage Mariusz Szczygieł and Wojciech Jagielski. A mentor for the BCLT's Emerging Translators' Mentorship Programme and Co-Chair of the UK Translators Association, she lives in London.

Czesław Miłosz, distinguished Polish-Lithuanian poet, prose writer and translator, won the 1980 Nobel Prize in Literature. With Leonard Nathan, he translated Anna Swir's *Talking to My Body* (Copper Canyon, 1996). For many years a professor of Polish literature in the Department of Slavic Languages and Literatures at the University of California, Berkeley, Miłosz died in Krakow in 2004.

Leonard Nathan was a poet, critic and professor emeritus of rhetoric at the University of California, Berkeley. The author of seventeen volumes of poetry, Nathan collaborated with Czesław Miłosz on the translation of Anna Swir and Aleksander Wat. He died in 2007.

Ewa Elżbieta Nowakowska is a poet, translator and essayist. Her translations of William Blake, Anne Carson, and Eugeniusz Tkaczyszyn-Dycki have appeared in American and Polish periodicals and anthologies. With Robin Davidson, she translated Ewa Lipska's *The New Century* (Northwestern, 2011).

Benjamin Paloff, Associate Professor of Comparative Literature at the University of Michigan, has translated the work of Dorota Masłowska, Marek Bieńczyk, and Andrzej Sosnowski. With Alissa Valles, he is translating Bożena Keff's *The Thing About Mother and Fatherland.* He's the author of two poetry collections, most recently *And His Orchestra* (Carnegie Mellon, 2014).

Alissa Valles is the editor and co-translator of Zbigniew Herbert's *Collected Poems 1956–1998* and his *Collected Prose 1948–1998.* A recipient of the Poetry Magazine Ruth Lilly Poetry Fellowship and the Bess Hokin Prize, Valles has worked for the BBC, the Dutch Institute of War Documentation, and the Jewish Historical Institute. She has served as an editor for the online journal *Words Without Borders.* She lives in Cambridge, Massachusetts.

Iza Wojciechowska received an MFA in creative writing from Columbia University with concentrations in literary translation and creative nonfiction. She is the recipient of a PEN/Heim Translation Award, and her translations of Anna Piwkowska's poetry have appeared in *A Public Space, Hayden's Ferry Review, Inventory, The Common,* and *The Massachusetts Review*. She lives in Durham, N.C.

Elżbieta Wójcik-Leese writes between English, Polish and Danish. Her translations of contemporary Polish poetry appear regularly in journals and anthologies. Her books incude *Nothing More/Więcej nic*, a selection from Krystyna Miłobędzka (2013); *Salt Monody,* versions of Marzanna Kielar (2006); *Cognitive Poetic Read-*

ings in Elizabeth Bishop: Portrait of a Mind Thinking (2010). She has co-edited *Carnivorous Boy Carnivorous Bird: Poetry from Poland* (2004) and co-written *Metropoetica. Poetry and Urban Space: Women Writing Cities* (2013).

Notes on the Poems

Page 37: Bożena Keff, "Lara Croft" - This poem is excerpted from Keff's *The Thing About Mother and Fatherland* (2008), a booklength poem cycle that views questions of post-Holocaust Polish-Jewish identity through a critical lens. Layering the Demeter-Persephone myth, Mississippi blues tropes, and popular cultural icons such as Lara Croft, Keff represents a fraught relationship between a mother who's a Holocaust survivor and her adult daughter, set against a backdrop of lingering anti-Semitism.

Page 38: Agnieszka Wolny-Hamkało, "Fragments of Maps" - The White Stork Synagogue, located in Wrocław, in southwestern Poland, opened in 1829, when the city was called Breslau and belonged to the kingdom of Prussia. The name was taken from an inn of the same name, which had previously stood on that site. During Kristallnacht, the interior of the building was destroyed. But the synagogue remained a place of worship until 1943, when the Nazis took over the building, and the synagogue's courtyard became a collection point for sending Jews to the extermination camps. After the war, the synagogue was in use through 1974, until the authorities expropriated it and gave it to the University of Wrocław. It was subsequently returned to the Jewish community. In addition to being used for worship, the synagogue now has also become a Jewish cultural center, in which performances and concerts take place.

Page 39: Agnieszka Kuciak, "Wroniecka Street Pool" - Poznań's New Synagogue, built in 1907, was converted into a swimming hall for soldiers by the Wehrmacht during World War II. It remained the city pool until 2012, and generations of children learned to swim there. The building is currently being renovated to serve as a Jewish cultural center.

Page 44: Mira Kuś, "Poetry of the Seven Veils" - In Polish, "Butt" is pronounced like "boot."

Pewex (short for Przedsiębiorstwo Eksportu Wewnętrznego "Internal Export Company") was a chain of hard-currency stores in communist Poland, which sold otherwise unobtainable Western goods and also Polish merchandise rejected for export.

Page 66: Krystyna Lars, "'I Dreamed I Collaborated,' Says Joanna S., Solidarity Activist from Stalowa Wola" - Stalowa Wola, a city in southeastern Poland whose name means "steel will," contained a large factory, where armaments were produced. In the 1980s, many workers from that factory participated in the Solidarity opposition movement. In 1988, the mill was the only maker of armaments to join the nation-wide general strike. In this poem, a Solidarity activist from that city has a nightmare in which she signs an agreement to collaborate with the security police.

Page 85: Krystyna Lars, "Soiree at the Czar's Plenipotentiary" - In 1823, the Czar's authorities, headed by one Count Novosiltov, clamped down on the various secret societies, including school organizations, flourishing in Polish Lithuania. It was through this police action that Adam Mickiewicz, the twenty-four-year-old author of *Ballads and Romances* (1822), a book of poems that heralded the beginning of the Romantic period in Poland, was sent into exile to Moscow. Other Lithuanian schoolboys were not so lucky, convoyed to Siberia or the Russian army. After several years of a fairly easy life as a schoolteacher in Russia, in 1829 Mickiewicz left the Empire for permanent exile in the West. In Mickiewicz's subsequent epic play *Forefathers' Eve,* the character Novosiltov reappears as the host of a magnificent debauchery. Afterwards he is carried off by devils.

In Lars' portrait, however, Mickiewicz has not only stayed in Russia, but has torn up his manuscript of *Forefathers' Eve* and joined in the feast at Novosiltov's. In short, he has become a collaborator and a hack. By presenting this alternative version of Mickiewicz, whose life has become so representative of insurrectionary Polish identity, Lars seems to dramatize the pressures to collaborate that confront any writer under a repressive regime.

Page 86: Krystyna Lars, "The Military Governor Contemplates the Statue of Adam M." - In rather genteel exile in Russia during the early 1820s, the historical Adam Mickiewicz, through the help of acquaintances, wrangled a post in a prep school in the resort city of Odessa. While there he traveled to the Crimea in the company of the chief military commander in southern Russia, General Witt. His travels occasioned the book *Crimean Sonnets,* which appeared in Moscow in 1826 and was quickly translated into Russian, enjoying great popularity and further entrenching Mickiewicz in favored circles until his unexpected flight to the West in 1829. The inscription on the plaque in memory of Lars's "anti-Mickiewicz" involves an ironic reference to Mickiewicz's epic poem published in 1834 *(Pan Tadeusz,* or, *Count Thaddeus)* and to the third part of *Forefathers' Eve*, published in 1832. Both of these works were strongly anti-Russian in character, and their publication burned any bridge that might have connected Mickiewicz with the Czarist regime. In Lars's poem, however, the contents of these books are most certainly innocuous. Their author has stayed within the bounds of Mother Russia, becoming institutionalized just as the real Mickiewicz was appropriated by communist hagiography in Poland's postwar period.

Page 87: Katarzyna Boruń-Jagodzińska, "The Literary Life" - Krakowskie Przedmieście is the Warsaw street where the Polish Writers' Union was located.

Lou von Salomé was for three years Rilke's muse and lover.

Page 92: Joanna Mueller, "Proofreading" - The first part of the poem alludes to three earlier poets: Leopold Staff (1878-1957); Cyprian Kamil Norwid (1821-1883); and Tadeusz Różewicz (b. 1921). Staff's "Foundations," written after World War II, was translated by Czesław Miłosz:

> I built on the sand
> And it tumbled down,
> I built on a rock
> And it tumbled down.
> Now when I build, I shall begin
> With the smoke from the chimney.

"Redakcja jest redukcją" [Redaction is reduction] is an oft-cited maxim of Norwid's, and *Zawsze fragment* [Always a Fragment] is the title of a 1999 book by Różewicz.

Page 94: Justyna Bargielska, "Avantourism" - Skierniewice is a town in central Poland, situated halfway between Warsaw and Łódź.

Page 188: Julia Hartwig, "Escaping One's Chores" - This poem alludes to Wisława Szymborska, Urszula Kozioł, and Ewa Lipska, who directed the Polish Institute on Am Gestade Street in Vienna from 1995-97.

Page 207: Julia Hartwig, "Justly" - Nikifor (1895-1968) was a Polish folk and "naive" painter. Violetta Villas (1938-2011) was a Polish pop singer, known for her abundant hair.

Appendix: Polish Pronunciation

This guide is for readers interested in knowing more about the sounds of Polish, even to pronounce the poets' names. Unlike English orthography, in which the vowel "a" can be pronounced thirteen different ways, Polish spelling is highly phonetic. In multisyllabic words, the stress is typically on the penultimate syllable.

a as in "f**a**ther"

ą is a nasalized vowel, similar to French ***on***

cz is a hard "ch" sound, as in **church**

ć is a softer "ch" sound, similar to the sound before the u in "si**tu**ation"

e as in "b**e**d"

ę is a nasalized vowel, similar to French ***in***, i.e., "vin"

i as in "mach**i**ne"

ł is like an English "w" sound, as in "**w**et"

ń is a softer n sound which always occurs after a vowel; if it comes after an "a" it sounds like the "ine" in "f**ine**"; after "i," it sounds rather like the "in" in "s**ing**"; after "o," it sounds like the vowel blend in "c**oi**n"

o as in "c**o**ld"

ó is an "oo" sound as in "sc**oo**t"

rz sounds like the “zh” in “plea**su**re”

sz resembles a hard “sh” sound in English, as in “**sh**ut”

ś is a softer “sh” sound in English, similar to the “ti” in “edi**ti**on”

u is like the “oo” sound in “c**oo**l”

w is like an English “v”

ż is a soft “zh” sound like the “g” in “**g**enre”

ź is a slightly harder “zh” sound like the “zh” in “**Zh**ivago”

www.ingramcontent.com/pod-product-compliance
Lightning Source LLC
Jackson TN
JSHW021415170426
101040JS00011B/122

* 9 7 8 1 9 3 5 2 1 0 8 2 5 *